PAMELA FREY

The Woman Who Picked Up Her Child

Creative and Transformative Healing from Childhood Sexual Abuse

To Heather:
Thank-you for an incredible
group! I hope this book may
help others you assist in
healing! *[signature]*

First published by Snow Angel Press 2022

First edition

ISBN: 978-1-7774940-0-1

This book was professionally typeset on Reedsy.
Find out more at reedsy.com

Contents

What Others Are Saying About This Book

Pamela Frey has written a compelling account of her healing journey from child sexual abuse. It is an intimate and heartbreaking story that shows how hearts are mended in a supportive and loving environment. The short chapters are signposts on the way, mapping the terrain that adult Survivors face as they seek to move on from the trauma of their past. The author shares hope with the reader using striking metaphors and through sharing photos of her artwork. Survivors of any type of abuse will find themselves in this book. The book provides insight for those who are trying to learn about the impacts of abuse, and the strength required to survive.

Carol Penner PhD
Assistant Professor of Theological Studies
Conrad Grebel College University

Pamela Frey's heroic story of childhood trauma and torture stands out as being one of the most horrific, as well as the most inspiring, I have ever heard— and I have heard many. The world has finally acknowledged that childhood sexual abuse exists, but there is still too little understanding of the true toll it takes on every facet of one's life. If you have experienced the devastating betrayal of childhood sexual trauma, or if you love someone who has, you will find wise understandings and helpful insights and strategies necessary for keeping hope alive. *The Woman Who Picked Up Her Child* offers the reader the kind of remarkable truths about childhood trauma that can set us free.

Barbra Graber MFA
Leader at Survivors Network
of Those Abused by Priests, Mennonite Chapter
and Founder of The Mennonite Abuse Prevention List

The Woman Who Picked Up Her Child is a powerfully raw depiction of the tremendously brave act of healing from childhood sexual abuse. Pam has captured the true essence of what a healing journey looks like in a captivating memoir-esque self-help narrative. Furthermore, she has included useful and practical tools to assist the reader in their own healing journey. She has bared her soul, celebrated her wins, expressed her setbacks, and conquered many of her demons. A captivating story of true strength and courage.

Kate McLeod MA RSW
Clinical Director and Individual Counsellor
C.A.R.E. Counselling and Coaching

Foreword

Pamela Frey's profoundly brave, insightful book is a remarkable account of her successful journey of healing from sexual torture experienced as a child in a Canadian Mennonite community. Survivors and therapists alike are invited to share in her therapeutic journey through her accessible, informative, and poignant short texts that vividly illuminate—through words and images—her highly-committed and creative engagement in the counseling process.

As a clinical psychologist who has been working with Survivors of child sexual abuse since the mid-eighties, I've been honored to be a therapeutic partner in Pamela's healing journey. I met Pamela in the fall of 2016 when she became a client within my private practice. Pamela came to our first therapy session with a desire to work on the abuse issues from her past and a passion to move into her future with a new awareness and sense of herself.

With unfailing commitment to her therapeutic process, Pamela learned to embrace her innocence, reclaim the right to speak and be heard, and believe that she is worthy of being supported in her healing. Pamela described our sessions as *intense*, emotionally exhausting, and at times exhilarating when she experienced significant insights, revelations, and therapeutic breakthroughs. Four years of focused dedication to her healing process, informed by a creative healing resource-creation process and related journalling process, has led to Pamela's authority on an exciting, creative arts- and mindfulness-informed healing practice.

This book started to take its form through Pamela's cumulative creative outputs—inspired and debriefed in our counseling sessions—and her journalling of the process and impact of this process. Pamela started coming to our weekly sessions with thoughts she wrote during the week. Her counseling sessions would build upon her written reflections and the creative pieces she made in clay, wood, stone, and snow. One piece described in the book was made of forty-five pieces of paper with memories of shame that no longer served her. She describes her action of consciously, physically, releasing the shame.

Ultimately—I don't know at exactly what point—it was evident that without consciously deciding to write a book, Pamela was writing a collection of healing memoirs. I began to realize the possibility of Pam writing a *book*, which soon became a part of her healing process, both in breaking the silence and in demonstrating the real and tangible creative processes of healing. The writing also began to provide increasing evidence of successful milestones along the path of her healing journey.

Pamela sheds light on the healing process with incredible details of what it means to not only survive but to begin to learn to thrive. The book is a series of small vignettes that describe the struggle of her innovative and creative processes of healing from abuse. *The Woman Who Picks Up Her Child* details how she worked in counseling to learn various skills and methods to return to her body, become present in the room, and remove herself from the threatening emotional spaces of the past that the dissociated self would become lured into. It was during these difficult sessions that we began to co-create plans for developing processes, mechanisms, rituals, and resources to support her healing and promote her safety between sessions. I would talk about a theory or concept and suggest a modality for Pamela to work with such as cognitive behavioral therapy, breath work, positive affirmations, visualization, and mindfulness practice.

I would also ask her what she thought would be helpful to address the immediate sense of vulnerability regarding intrusive images, triggers, self-harm thoughts, and so on. We'd co-create a plan for her homework for her to complete between sessions. Pamela would return to her next counseling session having created something tangible, such as a physical resource as described in her book to ground herself and move forward in her healing. Most astounding for its substantial nature, complexity, and creative design was the day Pamela returned to counseling with a wooden bridge she'd designed and built. Her chapter on the bridge is an illustration of the moment in time when she learned she wanted to live and began believing she was worthy of healing.

Her healing commitment and remarkable creative engagement in the development of healing resources—and her reflections on them—led to the creation of this book and to her desire to share this creative healing process with other Survivors. This is not a book primarily about the dark unimaginable betrayal of an innocent child; rather, this book is about one woman's remarkable therapeutic journey and her victorious release from her abusers.Based on first-person testimony, this is an inspirational book about the power and potential of individual Survivors to heal.

Pamela's healing memoir describes how she gains increasing insight and momentum as she works to break away from the immobilizing fear, terror, and punishing entrapment of an abuse that had previously defined and controlled her life. This is a book about how the purity of Pamela Frey's spirit was not stolen by her abusers, and how the healing of her wounded self was forged through four years of fighting to disclose and understand her abuse and its impacts on her life.

It's also about how Pamela marshaled her fiery wisdom and immense creative energies to illuminate her courageous pathway to healing. Pamela's book, *The Woman Who Picked Up Her Child*, is about one woman's ability to find a safe place to remember,to learn to externalize the responsibility for the abuse, to shift the shame and blame to the abusers, and to learn self-love. Pamela shares with great openness, courage,and literary skill how she found the strength to pick up her child out of the dark dangerous basement of her past and move forward together with her inner child into the present.

Pamela Frey's healing biography is written in a clear and compelling manner. She provides the reader with an insightful and inspiring map to healing the incest wound with important reflections on and insights about her creative, wise, and successful healing process. It has been my tremendous privilege to walk beside Pam and Little Pamela as a companion on their healing journey. As a registered psychologist who has been working with Survivors of child sexual abuse for over thirty years, I believe this book should be included in every self-help reading list for child sexual abuse Survivor's and every therapist's library. Pamela Frey gives new meaning to the clinical concept of working with the inner child. Therapists will learn a great deal from reading her account of the relational, creative, complex, and spiral process that is a demanding yet liberating process of healing from child sexual abuse.

    The Woman Who Picked Up Her Child is also a breathtaking first-person testimony of hope for Survivors.

~ Terry Mitchell PhD, C Psych
  February 2022

Dedication

This book is dedicated to my wife, my love, Colleen. You stuck with me through the toughest times and cheered me on along the way. I can't imagine having gone through this journey without you. Your love and support were life savers—literally.

I would also like to dedicate this book to Dr. Terry Mitchell. Since our first therapeutic session, we've worked together to heal parts of me so wounded and lost I honestly couldn't see the possibilities that would come out of the hard work of therapy. You did. You believed in me when I didn't. Your wisdom, compassion, insights, and guidance have been—and continue to be—precious gifts.

Preface

At first, I wrote this book for my eyes only. It was a journal of my thoughts and activities undertaken throughout my healing journey from childhood sexual abuse. Through these words, helped by my therapist and with support from my wife and cherished friends, it became more than just a way for me to express myself. It quietly—and yet boldly—became a book for Survivors who need help, understanding, reassurance, and creative ideas that will enable them to pick up their own child, to be free from the demons of their past, and to walk confidently, Warrior style, into their future.

The activities mentioned in this book were things I did for me, for my healing. If the same ideas work for you to further your own healing, then I am honored. If my creativity births new ideas for someone to proceed with their own healing, then my dream will have come true.

I've done my best to be honest, authentic, and raw with all parts of my healing to help other Survivors know that perhaps their wildest thoughts are not unfamiliar to others, that processes can help, symbols can heal, and rituals can mend the holes that our abusers left in our souls.

Each person's journey of healing is different, unique, and ongoing. I can promise you, however, we survived the hard stuff as children and although healing is painful, constantly up and down and back and forth, it is not impossible. Take this from someone who was certain that my little girl was destined to be alone and certainly was never to be picked up.

About the Author

Pamela Frey is an expert on healing in a creative and transformative way as this has been her personal journey and experience, which she shares with courage and authenticity in this book.

Pamela studied theater at Eastern Mennonite University and earned her Bachelor of Arts in English Language and Literature from the University of Waterloo. She performed comedy and improv across North America from 1990 to 1995. She's worked with children of all ages throughout her career in various settings from daycare to closed custody for youth. She is employed with the Waterloo Region District School Board as a Child and Youth Worker in a high school. Pamela resides in Waterloo, Ontario,with her wife, Colleen, and their dog, Sadie.

Besides writing and creating, Pamela enjoys spending time with her family, going on adventure walks with her four-legged companion Sadie, enjoying beach days with her daughter, and camping in the north whenever possible.

Acknowledgments

First, I wish to acknowledge my incredibly talented brother-in-law, Kerry Daly. I would never have been able to create the Bridge without his guidance, help, and direction, and his expertise in woodworking. With Kerry's help and calm spirit, I was able to work along with him; together, we made the Bridge.

Later in my healing journey, I approached Kerry about adding a screen door. Again, he obliged my wishes, helped me make the door, literally screened it in for me, and then attached it to where I wanted it on my structure. Mostly, thank you, Kerry, for making me feel safe in a place that could have been a trigger for me.

Thank you to my dear sister-in-law, Helen Theresa Daly. Throughout my healing journey, she sent me cards, emails of encouragement, and strength. Most often, she sent me pictures of fierce grizzly bears that made me feel protected during the most vulnerable and fragile times of my healing.

Thank you to my dear friend and soul sister, Barbra Graber. Our little girls are forever bonded because of their tragic, similar pasts. Our friendship today is bonded with the strength that each of us brings to one another through our Warrior fortitude and righteous wisdom.

Thank you to Dr. Terry Mitchell who funded the preparation of this book. I will forever be grateful for your generosity. Thank you for being on this journey with me. I am beyond-lucky to have you as a therapist and fortunate to work with you in such a connected, authentic way.

I would also like to thank Dr. Virginia McGowan, *McGowan & Co.: The*

Write Edit Group, for editing my book and mentoring me through the process of publishing. From the first time we spoke, I felt a connection and it's been a wonderful journey with you.

Thank you to my amazing daughter, Danikka Frey, for your love and encouragement to follow my dream of completing this book and sharing it with others.

Thank you to my kind and giving wife, Colleen Daly, for walking along and often holding me during this entire journey. Your unconditional love and support has often been my strength. You believe in me, encourage me, and want me to heal, grow, and be as strong a woman as I can. What more could I ask for in a partner? I love you.

I would like to thank Rebeka Ryvola for her gifted creativity and art work for the front and back covers of this book. Working with you was mind blowing in the way you worked at connecting with me and the sensitive subject of this memoir to make all my wishes, visions, and desires come true. You are truly authentic, caring, and beyond talented. Thank you!

The most important acknowledgment is this last one. I thank each and every Survivor who is brave enough to have picked up this book. May the strength of each of our stories help you in your healing so that not only will you have picked up this book but also your child. For it is then that you can truly become the Warrior that you always have been but that was dormant in you until now.

A Word to the Reader

This book describes my trauma of childhood sexual abuse and my personal healing journey; as such, the views, thoughts, and opinions expressed, and the experiences described, are mine and mine alone. My story is intended to be an educational and inspirational account for other Survivors of childhood sexual abuse.

I'm sharing it with you with the understanding that my book is not offering a professional service. The strategies and tools described may not be suitable for every situation, although it is my hope that this will encourage you to find your own creative, transformative healing path. I encourage you to seek the services of a competent professional to guide you in your healing.

1

The Time has Come

Wow. Forty-five recalled memories of shame. Forty-five! I had no idea...No idea that I was carrying all those feelings—those memories of shame and embarrassment—and yet, when I sat quietly, I recalled each one fairly easily. And so, like the force of waves crashing onto the shore,these memories, and all the shame and embarrassment attached to them, continued to force their way into my mind, holding me hostage for years.

At forty-eight, that's a lot of shame. That's a lot of weight to drag around and I'm tired. I'm tired of being a hostage to these memories and feelings. Tired of holding myself back from freedom. Instead of dreading the force of the next wave that slams shame at me, I want to welcome the beauty and peace that life also has. I want to stand at the shore and feel cleansed, embracing a new tide, new adventures. I don't want to be a slave to these thoughts. Some of these shameful events were choices I consciously made as a child, a teen, and then an adult. Some were not as clearly made or directly chosen.

Regardless, it's time to set myself free; it's time to say to my little girl, "It's okay you didn't tell anyone about Nelson and Wilmer. It's okay that you stole things. It's okay that you broke things in anger, in

1

frustration, in desperation. You were little.You wanted to be cared for, to be nurtured, safe, and validated, and sometimes you weren't. Release those feelings in the wind and let them blow from you."

To my teenage Pam, I want to say, "It's okay. It's okay that your pain ran so deep that you found unhealthy things to do, things that perhaps you felt were normal. You continued to crave attention—pure and loving, divine in nature. So, you did what you knew, right or wrong. But it's over now. It's time to let go."

It's time for *me* to breathe and release, to exhale the dark, deep shame and embarrassment, and inhale light, goodness, and mercy. Teenage Pam made mistakes. All teenagers do. That part is real. The part I believe is inadequate, manic, irrational, and slightly insane is no longer necessary to hold onto anymore. Let the wind take each memory of shame and blow them into the sky, soaring higher and higher, never to be seen or embraced by me again.

To adult Pam, I now say, "Your soul is tired. You carry a lot. You mentally beat yourself up to the point where you feel disgust and such shame for yourself. You feel embarrassment that runs so deeply you scarcely can speak or breathe the words out loud. It is time to set yourself free from this, from all this shame—this self-hatred and embarrassment."

I must. It, they—all this shame and embarrassment—that are holding me prisoner. I made mistakes, bad choices, and bad decisions. I lied. I hurt. I tried to make myself more validated, more authentic when, in fact, it did the exact opposite. This shame and embarrassment robbed me of all goodness and although not always consciously present, they now keep me chained to them so that I am sure to feel less valuable and unlikely to be authentic at all. But it is time. Time to release. Time to let go of more darkness. Time to emerge from the drowning ways and receive light, receive healing. It's there. Grab the light. Release the shame. Walk out of the darkness.

An Exercise in Letting Go

It was a warm day in the spring of 2018. I collected my forty-five memories/words of shame, got into the car with our dog Shea,[1] and had my partner, Colleen, drive me to a bridge just outside of Hawkesville, Ontario. It's a bridge we sometimes walked to as teens and hung out on when my friends and I skipped Sunday School. I have fond memories of laughing and joking around with them on that bridge.

As we pulled over to the shoulder of the road, just in front of the bridge, I collected my forty-five pieces of paper. Each had a memory or word that immediately took me to a shameful and embarrassing place within myself. I opened the car door and told Colleen I would be back. As I walked to the bridge, I could feel the breeze on my skin blowing my hair and kissing my cheeks. Perfect. The wind was perfect for my little exercise.

I stood at the rail of the bridge and looked out at the plains of fields; the river flowed under me and the blue sky was above. I separated one piece of shame from the collection of forty-five. I read it, put my hand up in the air, and let it go. It danced and bounced several times before the wind snatched it away and carried it to the water. I watched the paper as it floated down in the water and sailed away. Shame one of forty-five was let go. Forty-four to go.

Each time, I deliberately and carefully separate done word or memory of shame from the collection, read the word or phrase, raised my hand into the air, released it, and then watched it dance, dart, somersault, or scurry away with the force of the wind. It always found the water. It either swirled around in one place for a while or was swept away by the current.

I crossed the road to the other side of the bridge and continued the exercise of letting go of my shame. This time, when I saw one memory of shame floating in the water, I noticed that something else was there too. In the water below, a small muskrat had found my shame. It took

3

the memory of that piece of paper in its mouth with ease, snatching it up as though it was its fresh catch of the day. I smiled. Every part of nature in this exercise—the wind, air, water, and animals—was helping me release my shame.

I walked back to the car, paperless—and, I had to admit, somewhat weightless too. I'd just watched my memories of shame leave my hand to be captured by the wind, spiral into the water, and float away. I let them go. Those thoughts that pushed me more often than not into torment were drowning in the river.

As we drove away from the bridge—the bridge that represents freedom on more than one level—I told myself I was free from shame, hoping it was only the beginning of a freedom long overdue.

2

A Power Greater Than Me

The sadness flows through me today like a raging river. Days have passed since this familiar friend distanced herself, almost like she has left to never return with the same force. But she is here again: this sadness that wraps around me like cling-wrap on leftovers. I suppose this feeling is somewhat left over, too.

For decades I hid behind smiles, lies, and humor. But to become authentic, truly authentic, I must embrace the sadness and welcome her into my being once more. I feel sad for my little one, my tiny little girl who was so vulnerable, so innocent, and so alone. I've shifted from the disbelief of thinking that family members actually did this, to the reality those tortuous things happened to me, often, over many years. I'm held captive by this sadness; for the things I had to endure, for the "digging deep" to survive because of the evil that descended on and penetrated me. I am sad that my body, my precious, sexual being was abused in ways that make it difficult for me to breathe when I think of those things today. Places that should have been sacred in my body were raped, tortured, and mutilated. Sometimes I am sad for never being given the opportunity to experience my sexuality in a curious and innocent way.

I'm sad that, as a child, I was quickly enveloped in a fear that consumed my mind, paralyzed my body, and chained me to beliefs that all men were scary, not to be trusted, and to never to let my guard down around them, whether they are familiar or strangers. For example, I'm sad that when I drove in cars with men for whom I babysat, I had my hand on the door handle for quick escape if needed.

I'm sad because I was molded—not by choice but by my circumstances—to think my body was on this earth to feel pain so others received pleasure, power, and dominance. And, because of this, I embraced pain and found comfort and control when I invoked pain on myself. The adrenaline rush that came from bleeding, from the pounding blood at the surface of my skin, was a soothing balm and brought me peace.

Now I feel sad because I'm learning, within my innermost being, that pain is not comfort. Pain is not something I need to embrace. To me, the tears flow upon this discovery because, again, for decades, pain has been my friend. Hurting has been my companion. I'm sad because that's not what most children grow up learning, feeling, and experiencing. The salty tears flow down my cheeks, leaving trails of sadness, paths of tears cleansing my spirit from the false beliefs of my life. With this cleansing from toxic thoughts, I only hope the force within me that has embraced physical pain for so long does not win this war going on inside me. I do see this as a war. The war is between them and all of me—both Little and Adult Pamela.

Healing Imagery

As I stand at a cliff in my mind's eye, I call on Spirit to keep me strong. I have won battles in this war, but there are more to fight, many more thoughts to conquer. This battle to not harm is raging within my mind. My nemesis is pleading for victory, just one more time. And it's hard not to surrender. So damn hard.

On the cliff, I stand: a Warrior, fighting for my life, my freedom. Before me, I see a Raven swoop down. Its massive wingspan invites me to climb on. I get on with caution, not knowing where I'm going but sensing this is good, this is safe. The Raven gracefully lifts us up into the sky, cawing like a bird in battle. I cling to her feathers and nestle into the safety of her wings.

We fly higher; the cliff becomes smaller, less ominous, less fearful. I hide my face in the back of her neck, feeling her strength, breathing in her power. She continues to call like one in battle. We continue to fly.

The next thing I know, we are in a beautiful place. All is lush, full of color, and so peaceful. The Raven has stopped her Warrior cry. She descends upon this land of paradise. As she ever so gently lands on the earth, she turns her head so that, for the first time, her eye looks at mine. The wisdom I see, the depth to which she seems to penetrate deep inside my soul, does not cause me to fear, but somehow transfuses strength within me.

I slowly crawl off Raven's back and when I see myself, I am small, perhaps four, maybe five years old. I don't feel afraid, I feel powerful. I look around me and see water, a small brook nestled in between two blankets of grass. I walk toward this quiet, bubbling brook and crouch down, noticing my reflection in the clear water. I look calm, perhaps stronger. To my left, I hear the ruffling of feathers, then a gentle flapping of wings. Raven looks back, ever so slightly, but then with one loud caw ascends into the air, like a Warrior spirit celebrating victory with such clarity, strength, and grandeur. My small arm raises and waves good-bye to Raven who saved me from losing the battle against pain today. I skip along the edge of the brook, no longer fighting my demons. At least, for now.

3

Tossed Salad

I had a mental health day today. I needed to. Being at work made me angry and grumpy. I wanted to scream and cry. Everything set me into an electric buzz of anger. And then, in my passive aggressive way, I communicated with my colleagues. Not good. Not wise—and definitely not healthy. So, I am at home alone. Captured in my thoughts. They seem to have a hold on me these past few days like a wrestler has an opponent in a headlock or choke hold.

Sometimes I feel so much I can't separate my emotions. Inside my heart, it's like a tossed salad with so many feelings pulsing through my arteries. Other times I feel indifferent, almost numb. I suppose I'm depleted. I suppose my spirit is somewhat broken. I say "somewhat" because—somewhere in all this—I must be clinging onto some idea of hope, of freedom. It's difficult casting light on these dark shadows. I've never been a fan of the dark. Shadows rarely appear friendly.

I've mentioned the war I'm fighting, one that involves different battles to be fought throughout this journey. Today seems like the battle is inside my head and my spirit. My spirit is empty. My mind feels defeated and, yet, "the show must go on." I stand in the wings, feeling like it's mere minutes before the curtain rises. What will I see? What will my spirit need to prepare herself?Will the room be filled with my abusers, shame, embarrassment—dreams of a better future deferred? Will it reek with a pungent smell of hatred rather than the sweet aroma of love? Will I emerge from the wing and rise to the beasts of my past like a Warrior? Or will the fear consume me, leaving me floundering in the shadows of my past?

My worst battles in this war come from my head. The memories are excruciatingly painful, the reality of my torture and abuse devastating. But making peace with this—finding, reaching out for, and embracing my tiny little one—is the hardest battle by far. Two steps forward, three steps back. Today, I want to walk out of the wings, but somehow my feet remain cemented to the floor.

Shahida Arabi wrote, "Time or words alone can't always soothe the wounds that can't be put into Language."[2] You know, I believe that's true. It's like sometimes this trauma is coming at me in a different Language. It has crawled inside every part of me and I try, I try *so damn hard* to decode it, figure it out, and somehow make sense of the pain, the memories, the woundedness that words can't seem to translate from my body. But then, I feel sad. I feel sad and salty tears flow from my eyes.

Immediately following the tears, my mind starts with the negative tapes: "Get over it. Many people have had it worse. You're fine, you're safe,and you're functioning. Just stop. Stop it!" Embarrassment follows and then the shame. I feel like I should be moving on. That's when my mind has taken a dagger to my heart and the score is Mind 1, Spirit 0.

I've been told that healing has no formula. There's no magic remedy, no timeline. It's not a linear method of theories and words. Rather, it's a painful journey of distortions; secrets never spoken; scabby, festering wounds; smoke and mirrors. My therapist says that healing can't be measured. She says it peaks and dips, and that sometimes I will and have walked out from the wings, and sometimes I haven't or won't. I'm starting to believe she may be right. I suppose I want her to be.

But what if I can't heal and I stay on this journey for a lifetime? What if I'm in an abyss too deep to be helped or rescued? What if I'm too tired to care? Arabi also writes,

> But rest assured that one day in the future there will be the privilege of more awakenings and of more happiness than you can capture in photographs: new growing pains and new first drafts. Rest assured that if you do not give up now, you'll get the chance to change the course of everything that's still unwritten.[3]
> [2]

Dr. Mitchell and Arabi could be friends. I think they theorize in similar ways. I believe they live practicing this theory. If only I could practice this theory! Then perhaps I could emerge from the fog, this chrysalis that is suffocating me...for then, I too, could be free.

With shaky missteps, I'm learning to walk instead of crawl—even though today the floor seems safer and walking—even holding onto others for support doesn't seem possible. Today I sit with this tossed salad of emotions.

4

My Body Knows Something

Another mental health day. I have such a bad headache—a migraine so bad that, even with my medication, I can't tackle the thought of going to school. I feel out of sorts. The feeling is like everyone around me is "on the same page" and I haven't a clue as to what book they're reading! I don't know what to think or say to others. It's like when I'm going down the hallway at school and everyone is going the opposite way as me. I feel uncomfortable, misplaced, lost.

I don't like how I'm feeling: absorbed in my own thoughts, waiting for something. What *is* that thing? What am I waiting for? A revelation? An epiphany? Some kind of "ah-hah" moment where all things make sense? I don't like being in my own skin right now. I feel agitated, bothered, unsettled. I look at my left forearm tattoo and read my mantra: *Eunoia*. It means "beautiful thinking, connoting a well-balanced mind." But I don't feel balanced and I sure am struggling to think beautiful thoughts.

Sometimes I just want to disappear and go far, far away. That feels like a beautiful thought right now. However, I don't know what that would accomplish, and that's the problem. I feel like I don't know anything. I don't know how to speak my thoughts, identify my feelings, or even know what I want! I HATE THIS! It's a horrible feeling to be so unsettled, so lost and scattered.

When I'm at work, I feel unhappy, angry, and disjointed. When I don't get what I want, I feel like tantrumming. My co-workers must feel like they need to walk cautiously around me, measuring their words, so I don't "snap" with my responses.

I hate it when I'm like this. I can't seem to connect with my creative energy. I want to do some free writing and I can't attempt to connect with Spirit: where is She? I can't see Her, I can't hear Her, and I certainly can't connect with Her through my spirit. As a result, I'm left empty, alone. I'm not alone physically, however. My partner Colleen is here, wanting me to share. The thing is, I don't know what to say. Not even writing is helping and it usually does. The weather is gray, cold, blah. My spirit feels the same. If I could just connect with something, some symbol of hope, of brighter days...

Creative Imagery

Once again, I find myself at a cliff. This time, I'm sitting on the edge, my legs dangling, my body slumped, my eyes looking out at my surroundings. The sky is blue, a sprinkle of white clouds are suspended in various places in the vastness above me. I can't see the sun, but I feel her warmth as it kisses my skin so gently.

I feel sadness within my heart, a sense of hopelessness. I breathe in the quiet solitude around me. My spirit tries to connect with the vastness around me, like the hope an empty canvas has when mounted on an easel before an artist.

A warm breeze sweeps around me, stirring up the light dirt where I sit. I watch the swirls the dust makes, being lifted from its place, ever so slightly blown to a new resting spot. I suppose that's how I feel. I've been so sedentary in my life with my past abuse. Like the dirt knows the wind, I know my past, but until these last six or seven months, I didn't let the memories move me. I battened myself down, unable to revisit the horrors that happened to me. But now, now I have. I'm like dirt that whirls around in the wind, making a new place, finding a new home within myself.

I've never been a big fan of the wind. It blows things we don't want on to us and around us. It scatters things for us to retrieve. Where I was before this tempest tossed may have felt safe, but it wasn't. It wasn't safe because *they* had the power. *They* kept me from moving. *They* held me down. Until now.

Now, with all the things I feel and don't feel, with the things I know and don't know, I move on. It might be from huge gusts of winds: memories strong and powerful. It might be from gentle breezes, moments where things are stirred that cause unsettled feelings. I move on.

Eunoia may not be on this cliff with me right now. It may not be tomorrow or the next day either. Like the dirt that whirls around me, orchestrated by the wind. I too am whirling, trying to find a new home within me where Little Pamela and I are safe and free.

5

Ax Throwing and Sand Sculpting

Homework from my therapist: Have fun, relax. Enjoy the break and indulge in self-care.

Wow! For some, that may seem easy. For me, it's a work in progress, at least for my mind. But I'm getting better at it. I'm gaining tools and finding strategies that help me put *me* first in healthier ways than the ones I usually tap into.

When I look back from where I began therapy to where I am now, I see how I've grown. I've climbed up the spiral of healing, sometimes at great speed. I've also fallen a number of times down the spiral. But when I'm further down, it's not as scary, unfamiliar, and dark as it used to be. With my new strategies and tools, I'm much more capable of climbing back up again. Today, at this moment, I feel good energy. I feel strong and powerful.

I went ax throwing yesterday! It was amazingly cathartic and so gratifying! I called it Operation NW, which is code for the first initials of my abusers. God, did I throw the ax at the target—in this case, targets! I hit the bull's eye at least three times, and the target itself almost always. The rush of adrenaline from the anger I let loose gushed out from every pore in my body and it was exhilarating!

Anger truly is another form of energy. I've been afraid to get angry until my dear friend and fellow Survivor, Barbra, taught me to think of anger as simply a flow of energy. She told me I won't get stuck in a rage; rather, it's the people who don't express anger or rage who end up in mental hospitals or even dead from the buildup of their rage and anger. I hung onto that during ax throwing. Anger flowed through my body easily. I didn't rage or lose control. I channeled that energy in a focused,clear, concise manner. With each ax I threw, I fought for Little Pamela. I hacked at those perpetrators until they were absolutely incapable of damaging her, coming close to her, or ever hurting her again. I beat those men with an ax and I saved Little Pamela. And. It. Felt. Good. No, it felt empowering, inspiring, and liberating.

How did I plan to have fun this week? How did I relax and take breaks? I did it through the amazing sport of ax throwing! Who knew?

After ax throwing, I went through our home and smudged every room, every place where I've ever cried or remembered my abuse. That was cleansing. Through this ritual, I felt such positive and healing energy flow through me. I then took my sculpting sand and made Little Pamela sitting on a tiny bench: happy, calm, and peaceful. Beside her, I sculpted an ax to help her to remember "I got the bad guys for her." She's safe. She can truly feel protected.

I also sculpted a bunny. Rabbits are fun to watch. I have several of them in my backyard that come out on a daily basis. I enjoy watching them. Sometimes, they freeze and stare at me, probably wondering if I'm safe. At other times, they hop pretty close to me and nibble away at any grass that may need manicuring. My favorite times are when I see two of them playing together, chasing each other in and out of the bush, up and down the yard. They are so quick and carefree.

The sculpting was fun and made me smile. Ax throwing was healing and empowering. Smudging helped positive energy flow through me and around me. I am healing. I am growing. I am stronger.

15

6

First Come, First Served

I'm off work, resting, relaxing, and taking care of my little girl. I'm choosing to believe that this "Leave of Absence" symbolizes putting me first. It's a significant action for me to say, "No matter what child I feel may need me at school, I come first. " And it feels oddly gratifying to be off work. I wasn't sure what I'd feel like—what the time would be like—but I feel like I'm breathing better, thinking more clearly, and struggling less with keeping my emotion sin check.

However, I was going to help a colleague by attending a field trip on Friday and I totally messed up because I got a text this morning asking if I would be there today. The actual trip is happening as I write! My heart sank when I got the text and yet, strangely, not as deeply as perhaps it would have in the past. I felt badly that I mixed the days up and let the teacher down when I said I'd be there and wasn't. I don't think it ever feels good to disappoint a friend, but when I stopped to think about the kids who were counting on seeing me and being in my group, I knew they'd survive. I was okay with my mistakes even knowing their uncertainty about the trip and the anxieties that come with anticipating the unknown. I think, somewhere deep inside me, Little Pamela was relieved because having made this mistake, she is still first. Other children don't come before her.

My breathing becomes lighter—and yet strangely, deeper. No inter-ruption is created by putting other kids first and making her wait, again. Little Pamela didn't have to wait for her turn to be first, to be gently cared for. It's quite liberating, this idea of being first. I've not tried to protect anyone during this leave from work except myself. I'm starting to believe true freedom comes from this type of self-kindness. Hmmm. What a concept: to practice myself what I've been encouraging so many others to do for years—especially women!

Here I am into Day Three of Mental Health Leave, not worried about how things will unfold for me, not worried about how to take care of Little Pamela, because consciously—and even unconsciously—I'm taking care of her. She is here, in my presence: first in line, first to be served, and first to be listened to. And it feels good, peaceful.

7

Retribution

During my time away from school, I thought a lot about how or when the fear of my abusers began to dissipate. I've been thinking of the word my therapist used: *retribution*. She asked me if I felt any retribution after ax throwing. As I thought about it, I could honestly say I didn't. Driving away from that session. and now weeks after, I've thought about that question often.

I looked up definitions of the word retribution. The second and third definitions given in Merriam-Webster's online dictionary are the ones I thought about most:

#2. *The dispensing or receiving of reward or punishment, especially in the hereafter.*

#3. *Something given or exacted in recompense, especially punishment.*[4]

For decades, I've lived in fear that *if I looked deeply into my past*, healed my wounds and memories of abuse and torture, and "stared" my abusers in the face, something horrible would happen *to me or my loved ones.* I remember being filled with terror if I thought about speaking truth as a little girl; a crystal-clear image of having to either shoot my mom or myself would enter my mind.

I hated that thought. I hated the feelings that came with those thoughts. I always pictured turning the gun on myself and saving my mother. But the feeling of fear was the worst of that whole memory. The sheer terror of *getting caught* by them was horrifying. I'm starting to believe that the terror I lived with wasn't typical; that for some reason (and now I know why) I lived in constant Fear, even as a little girl, always watching behind my back, always being hyper vigilant. I did this everywhere, for fear that something bad would happen to me if I spoke the truth, if I talked or did something wrong. I'm coming to understand that although that was "my normal" from a very early age, to be in a state of constant fear is not the norm for most people.

I lived in conscious fear of retribution and I didn't know it back then. I didn't understand that I wouldn't be healed until I broke free from the thoughts and beliefs that chained me for decades. As a little girl, I suppose retribution was more defined for me by the third definition: something given or exacted in recompense, especially punishment. If I spoke the truth, I would die. I believed that with every cell of my being.

In my teens and adult years, when I developed more rational thinking, I focused on the second definition: retribution from my abusers in the hereafter. I was seventeen when Fear shifted from "I would die" to terrible things would happen to me: curses would be put on me if I spoke about the abuse. I would suffer! The irony of that belief is *it* created so much suffering and so much pain. In carrying that belief, I'd sometimes explode with confusion and anger. To self-harm was the only way I could release whatever I was feeling or didn't want to feel. Sadly, self- harm became the "go to" release: self-retribution to ensure my silence. And then...

I met the most intelligent, wise, caring, and helpful therapist. And ever so slowly, I began to release the Fear of my abusers' retribution. I began to understand how my abusers brainwashed me into silence by keeping me in a constant state of Fear and that Fear grew into sheer terror so I never stopped believing—even when they died—that retribution would catch up with me. I didn't stop believing that retribution would be mine if I spoke.

In the safety and gentle presence of Dr. Terry Mitchell, I started to speak the truth. Fear was there, its presence lingering like a predator stalking its prey; but in my healing, I kept talking. Dr. Mitchell and other loved ones kept themselves between me and that Fear. I still saw it, felt its presence, but with no retribution from it. Slowly, I started understanding what safety was. I wasn't alone in my thoughts. I'd spoken the truth and was being cared for. That care was through my therapy sessions, in the arms of Colleen, during phone calls to Barbra, and when looking into my sister's eyes, knowing she knew full on because she had lived through and survived a lot of what I had. Fear was becoming smaller. Light, love, and safety were growing.

Somewhere in the process of nurturing those feelings, watching those emotions sprout inside of me, I felt brave enough to try ax throwing and experiment with what it might feel like to direct some of the anger and darkness carried from my abuse by projecting it onto a target using an ax. Wow! It was invigorating. Empowering. Safe. And mostly, even after going a couple of times and planning to go again, there has been no retribution from my abusers.

I wish I could say the Fear that's eaten away at my mind and guts is gone, but it isn't. The good news is that as light, love, safety, and self-nurturing rise up within me, Fear is losing power. And I'll continue to brave this storm with courage and the belief that I'm not alone. A gathering of strong women have circled around me like a posse, ready to care for me when I can't do that myself. Just knowing I have people around me to care for me oddly gives me strength to do that myself, in better and healthier ways.

I suppose if I feel any retribution from speaking the truth, it's that whenever I see older men with little girls doing any one-on-one activities, I immediately wonder whether that little girl is safe or is being abused and is silently suffering. If I see anger or sadness in children, I immediately think they may be being abused and are trying to tell but can't because Fear has captured their soul and is keeping them silent. I put pressure on myself to be their voice, their protector or savior.

I'm on medical leave right now. I've stepped out of my role as a child and youth worker to take care of Little Pamela. I'm doing so because it is what I need to do. Fear of retribution is slowly being choked out of my life.

Today, I'm grateful.

8

They Don't Fool Me!

They sit in their pews with their righteous smiles pasted on their faces, masking the evil that lies within. They walk around the community offering to help those who need repairs, renovations, or new items constructed, hiding the heinous crimes they commit under their kindness and generosity. It doesn't fool all of us. It doesn't fool *any* of us that know the ugly monsters that come forth when they are with little girls.

This man, Wilmer, has disgusting secrets: deeds he perpetrated on small, innocent girls. He was a Mennonite farmer who worked on the farm that was originally my maternal grandfather's, the farm where my mother and her family grew up. He performed acts with cows that no one should see. He made a little girl watch him have sex with a cow in the basement of a dirty, dusty barn. He propped her up on a ledge and faced her toward the cow and his excited self. His smile was no longer hiding the evil, no longer appearing kind or righteous. He became a monster to that little girl. As he performed this indecent act, he stared at that little girl, smiling. As if forcing her to watch was not evil enough, he stepped down from his perch and proceeded to take the innocent but now terrified child to a calf pen full of dusty straw and hay. This man put her face first down on that straw, pulled down her panties, lifted her dress, spread her legs far apart, and sodomized her for what seemed like an eternity. I know this evil that Wilmer hid from the Mennonite church, the family, and the community.

I know.

On another occasion, this same monster lifted this sweet child up to the mouth of a cow. He pulled her panties down. She felt his hot breath, permeated with evil, and exhaled a pungent mist of vile hatred against her face. He made the cow lick that little girl's vagina for what must have felt like forever. And then, this man proceeded to digitally rape her. He did not speak. He did not have to; his eyes were violently clear that with the heinous acts he did, this child must stay silent or terrible things would happen. Although she did not speak, her spirit was screaming, her body was shattered.

Another older man named Nelson was the little girl's biological, maternal grandfather. He was not grand. He was not a father. He was Dr. Jekyll and Mr. Hyde. Nelson was quiet and soft spoken. He seemed kind when he took the little girl's hand and led her to the shed.

A shaft of natural light split the darkness through a crack in a dirty window.

He lifted her onto a rickety old table. The little girl trusted him. He told her to lie down on her back. He lifted her dress; he took off her panties. His eyes changed. He didn't look kind anymore. He did not speak, nor did she. Nelson moved a bucket of water beside the table. A rag floated in the pail. His massive hands grabbed a bunch of tools beside him. He took these tools, one by one, and inserted them into this little girl's vagina and anus. The little girl had tears and the little girl felt pain, but he did not stop. When there was blood, he took the rag and wiped it away from between her legs. The little girl turned her head and looked at the bucket on the floor beside the table. The water had turned pink.

The little girl looked like she was sweating, trying to escape the forces that caused this pain through the violent acts done by this man. The girl's eyes looked like glass.They didn't look like they could see anything. They didn't have to because she had already seen enough. And what she felt, what cut her, penetrated her, harmed her, and tortured her little body would never, ever be erased. Those images were branded into her being for life. But he just cleaned her up, lifted her off the table, reassembled her dress and panties, and led her back quietly to where she had been plucked from.

The little girl hurt from the inside out. It was hard for her to walk. Later,out of the monster's view, she bled, she cried, she curled up into a ball, holding her breath, trying to move out of the experience she had just endured. She did, but only to have that man, that evil monster come and take her hand again and again on different days, penetrating her, raping her with tools.This man had evil eyes. During those times,he did not hide behind kindness and generosity. He let that monster out because he WAS THAT MONSTER.

Nelson and Wilmer were evil monsters and tried to hide it with goodness.

They didn't fool me.

9

The Bridge

Many steps—literally and figuratively—are taken before acute healing takes place. For some, the steps are quick, rapid; for others, they are slow and steady and can take years. My steps to the pain, the horror of looking at and healing my abuse, were slow, steady steps.

I stood in front of a door that was the gateway to the intensity of my abuse but also the opening to a new life of freedom. The door was difficult to open, but it did have a window. When I looked through it, I could see the pain, the agony, that lay ahead of me. It needed to be my choice: I could push that door open or continue to look through the window, but the latter choice would limit me in so many endless ways.

I chose.

Immediately upon opening the door and walking through the doorway, I found a drop down to the path of a Bridge...I had no choice but to leap to it if I wanted healing—if I wanted freedom.

I took a while to take that jump because it looked scary and foreboding. Although it wasn't a huge leap like a standing long jump, the distance felt far because I knew what I was jumping into. And yet, really, I had no idea.

When I took that leap into whatever lay ahead, it wasn't too bad.

However, it didn't take long for me to notice that the Bridge to healing did not have solid footing. The Bridge, my Bridge of Healing, was up and down, almost like a roller coaster. At times, the footing was unbearable. Each step was a different width and durability, and the space varied between each one. When I looked between each foothold, I saw black holes emptying into an abyss of darkness and impending doom. There were moments on that Bridge where my footing was so uncertain and precarious, my future so terrifying and my present so unmanageable, that I didn't know how I would put one foot in front of the other.

But I did. I saw people on the Bridge who supported me—who believed in me and my healing journey to freedom—even more than I believe I ever did. When I was in what seemed like the lowest, deepest, darkest moments crossing the Bridge, when I felt like I wanted to fall into the abyss of darkness, I was encouraged to keep my footing, hold on, and forge ahead. That meant not only looking at and reliving the abuse from my past but making some kind of peace with it. I'd never accept it, but I'd learned to acknowledge it.

But the abuse is not *my* story. It's *their* story and they pulled me into it.

Because of that, I have lasting memories. I've had to embrace heart-wrenching pain and I've had to face truths that, for the longest time, I carried as shame in my life. With each painstaking and sometimes precarious step, I started to see that the shame from being abused is not mine to carry. It is the Abusers. The shame of being abused runs to the depth of my soul, but I am starting to see, to recognize, that I do not need—nor do I deserve—to carry any blame. It is not mine. It is theirs. Some days I step with confidence in knowing that; on other days, those steps feel shaky and uncertain. Regardless of the steps, regardless of the ups and downs the Bridge holds, I've kept moving forward, determined to reach the other side. I'm not there yet, but I'm closer and more confident than ever that freedom is mine to behold.

When journeying across the "highs" on my Bridge,I glimpse freedom and feel moments of hope, so I travel on. Someday, I want to reach the other side and stay there. There are posts for me to grab hold of at the end of the footpath on the Bridge. I will grab hold and, someday, will pull myself off the Bridge and stay off of it once and for all. I suppose I'll always live with the Bridge as part of me, but I choose to believe I don't need to remain there any longer than necessary.

10

And...Cut

For someone who has never deliberately self-harmed, I think cutting is hard to fathom. Cutting is control, release, and punishment—at least for me. When something in my life scares me, makes me feel I have no power or control over a situation, I immediately want to cut. I want to do something I have control over. I want to feel the rush in my body when my tool of choice divides the skin. I embrace the release I feel when I watch the blood drip from my cut. In that moment, I feel power and more control than I did before cutting.

When I feel afraid, unsafe, or that I have done something "wrong," the urge to cut comes over me like waves that crash into rocks on a shoreline. The voice inside my head beckons me to find a blade and slice the terror, the flaws, away. If I cut and bleed and it stings or throbs, I'm no longer a slave to Fear. Failure and powerlessness cease to subconsciously beat me. Rather, I've taken control. I've driven terror out of its perch in my mind and I've taken over residence with my thoughts.

How long between cuts? That depends—sometimes hours, days, weeks, months. I even managed years at one point. Not right now. Not with what I'm dealing with. So, I cut. I cut when my heart hurts and I can't even begin to put my pain into words. I cut when I feel inadequate and undeserving. And I cut when I'm afraid: afraid of a multitude of things, situations, people, "what ifs?," and my past.

Cutting is neither a healthy tool, nor is it a healthy strategy to use. It's not the answer, the "go to" solution. Cutting brings momentary release and control but burns a trail of worry, shame, secrecy, and scars after each and every slash carved into my skin.

Helped by my support system—my psychologist and closest allies—I'm exploring new ways to cope. Some days, I can choose healthier ways and coping strategies; on other days, the feelings come raging at me with such force that I embrace the darkness.

Self-harm is similar to an addiction, I imagine. Or it can be. Like a recovering alcoholic wrestles with the urge to grab their next drink, my fight is against wanting to grab the sharpest knife or blade and make the next cut.

Please understand. Those of us who struggle with self-harm of any kind are not doing it to hurt our loved ones. We're silently struggling and suffering. We're not vying for attention. We're trying to learn new strategies. We're trying to invent new tools that teach us to love ourselves and to embrace all parts of our souls. But the darkness lingers, coupled with the eerie, haunting summons to gash, pierce, or cut.

If you are a cutter, you aren't alone. I'm with you. I understand the battle, the shame, the lies, the release. However, there are healthier ways to deal with the pain, shame, stress, fear, inadequacy, and self-hatred. One step forward...one confidant who loves unconditionally... one knife down...one breath at a time.

11

Words

Words.

Words can lift us up, comfort us, empower us, and build confidence.Words can trap us, trick us, terrify us, change us, and haunt us. Words are often used as mantras branded into our psyche to draw on in times of need. Those words are powerful but so are the negative ones we carry in our souls that become our core beliefs—the words that devour us in the night, taunt us in a crowd, and hover over us like a swarm of bees waiting to attack.

Survivors have a lot of words, phrases, and lies that can take a long time— sometimes a lifetime—to unpack, discover the truthful words, and heal. Words can be as powerful as the acts of abuse and torture. Offenders are stellar at knowing what to say to tattoo their voice along with their fear and power into the minds of their victims with the choice of their words.

The words that injured me along with the sexual abuse, the ones that have such power, seem to take forever to break free from. These words that lodged themselves into my mind and my heart are words like *Shame, Self-doubt, Unworthy, Unclean, Broken,* and *Incapable.* Powerful words. Words that have imprisoned me most of my natural life. Each one in its own unique way can paralyze me on any given day in any given situation.

Let me begin with Shame. Most people have experienced Shame at some point or time. Shame can often melt away from a situation through forgiveness, explanation, apology, or perhaps even time. But how does a Survivor relieve herself from the pain left behind by Shame? It feels impossible. It feels like a constant uphill battle with little reprieve from the fight. The Shame I feel is the master of all the words that grip so tightly around my mind. It has so brilliantly wrapped itself around my brain like a web spun to catch its next victim, sucking the blood—the life—victoriously from the kill. Shame is my master word because from Shame is birthed Self-doubt, Worthlessness, feeling Unclean, Broken, and then, of course, Incapable. When Shame dominates, I cower in the shadow of her monstrosity. I feel undeserving of anything. If I don't believe in myself, which is synonymous for low self-esteem, then right on the heels of feeling incompetent come their descendants, Unworthiness and Brokenness, finished off with a powerful shot of Incapable.

The word Unclean connotes vivid thoughts in my mind without any effort at all. I simply go back in my mind and choose any one of my abusive experiences and feel Unclean. With Unclean being so real and so raw, the thought and belief saddle up perfectly with the word Broken. If I'm dirty, I'm unworthy. If I'm unworthy, I feel Broken. How do you fix thoughts of being Unclean? It's not like a shower or hot bath can wash the ick away. If a pressure washer could do the trick, I think most Survivors would own one! Although water can be a wonderful way to purify, a way to become almost reborn, water can't fix *this* Unclean and can't restore *this* kind of Broken.

I'm beginning to believe that healing from words happens in small doses, like the haze one might feel when beside waterfalls as a breeze comes and sprinkles fairy mist across your skin, into your pores. Sometimes you see the mist; most often you feel it first.

I've felt my demon words' adversaries and experienced that magical fairy mist challenge my core beliefs. When I've truly grasped—albeit fleetingly—that my offenders carry the shame, deserve the shame, I feel pride. I feel like a queen who has taken back her rightful land. When I accomplish something that I've struggled to fight off, like cutting, I feel strong and my esteem is that of a Warrior Woman ready to take on any battle set before her.

I *have* felt clean. I've felt clean when my therapist and support people still chose to love and care for me even after hearing about the terrible things I endured. My mind plays tricks on me with this one. I don't stay feeling this way long, but when I do, I don't feel Broken. I feel like I have the power of Joan of Arc. Give me any negative words and I'll conquer them with womanly power and strength.

When that happens, I feel Victorious, I feel Worthy, I feel Capable. In these times, words are letters that form whatever I want them to, whatever I deem worthwhile and significant.

Words. They can build you up. They can tear you down and destroy you. One thing I know for certain is they can take a lifetime to fight, decades to heal, and a lifetime to learn to avoid or embrace.

12

Reframe That Thought

Another day. Another point in time when choices need to be made, decisions determined, words monitored, feelings felt, and healing sought. In the rush of each day that brings demands from everyday routines to the extra stressors that life seems to unselfishly bestow, it's hard to be constantly aware of my personal journey to heal the hell I endured as a small child.

I'm trying to be mindful of the strength I continue to find within myself and choose to do healthy things for my body and mind. That feels like a full-time mental job!!!!

Being an experienced child and youth worker in a behavioral class,[5] it's not uncommon for me to need to contain students. This is a difficult part of my role on any day but, during my healing, I found it particularly difficult. How does one contain a child due to their aggression, self-harming behaviors, or attempts to harm others, and then seek healing? When I am containing a child—usually with two other adults—I don't find this to be healing. Seeing the child struggle beneath our holds, watching tears roll down their faces, and hearing the screams echoing in my ears does not create an atmosphere of healing for anyone—let alone my small, vulnerable, hurting, girl child.

Containments make me feel angry because it's not right to apply force on any human being, especially children, in such a physical way. I also feel afraid.Afraid of the damage we are doing to the psyche of that child. As at least two, usually three, adults are performing the containment to "protect" the child, I silently wonder what we're destroying in the meantime. I immediately dissociate; I once again sever my feelings to cope with my reality.

I remember my struggle to try to keep my legs together and having them split apart with force. I remember hot, salty tears rolling rapidly down my face with no one there to wipe them away, no one there to hold me and say, "You know what? What happened to you is horrible. I am here to save you. You will never, ever have to go through this again."

While dissociating from my own pain, I immediately seep through the pores of that poor child of whom we are demanding compliance. I search for their broken spirit, desperate for my little girl to reach theirs, to hold them tightly as two kids cling to each other for their lives in terrifying and hostile situations.

I feel empty, alone, when I look down and see one adult on each arm and a third adult holding the child's legs. I felt empty and alone after my legs were pried open and dirty, vile things were done to me. Is that what I do to these little spirits? The thought of hurting these children, damaging them again and again, makes me sick, physically ill.

Then, I reframe it with my therapist. Physical containments are not evil, vile, forceful acts done in secret to fulfill some sick adult's desire. Containments are a last resort when no other strategies are working and the student is at risk of harming themselves or others. I don't seek students to inflict pain on them. When I am involved in a containment, my voice is calm,and my desire is to help them, not hurt them. I'm not a perpetrator and they aren't my victims. I am a Child and Youth Worker and they are students. Although containments aren't pleasant and are a last resort, we aren't evil seeking to harm the children in our care.

Reframing is a huge part of healing from abusive memories and thoughts; it ensures that when one slips into a transference of thoughts or beliefs, one can start (with the help, in my case, of a therapist) to reframe incidents, beliefs, and thoughts, and hear the healthy voice, the mature, reasoned adult voice that can keep your inner child safe.

13

Healing is Not a "To-Do" List

I wish healing was a "To-Do" list. I'm pretty sure I thought healing my past would be like a to-do list in that I would have my therapist give me assignments— things to do, projects to work on—and BAM! I would be healed!

Initially, I worked hard on my imaginary list. My therapist would suggest something and I'd create a "job." I worked on many chapters in *The Courage to Heal* by Ellen Bass and Laura Davis,[6] thinking my healing will be complete when I'm done with the book and working with my therapist, even though different people (even the authors of *The Courage to Heal*) said it's not about completing each chapter and suddenly things would be better. Somehow, I thought I'd be different.

I worked diligently, and at times painfully, through that book. I made a collage as suggested by my therapist: one that would symbolize what I wanted in 2017. Check that off the list.

I worked with sand clay, molding out horrific memories and moments of my sexual abuse and torture. I then destroyed those creations, taking power back from what happened to my little girl. Check that off the list.

I made snow angels connecting me through play with my little girl. I put band-aids on all the parts of my body that were violated and hurt to symbolize caring for and soothing the pain and wounds of my childhood. I wrote lists of the memories where I carried shame for decades around my heart like chains. Then I took those lists, wrote each word on an individual piece of paper, and released them into the wind, watching the river below swallow them up, taking them from me, and setting me free. Shame, gone. Check that off the list.

I bought shells and secretly placed them around my neighborhood hoping a child would find one when they needed a piece of beauty in perhaps a less than happy life. Giving hope to others in my process of healing: check.

I went ax throwing to direct my anger and hatred at a target. The power in those moments when picturing those evil men who abused and tortured me was like nothing I'd experienced before or since. Dealing with my anger: check it off the list.

I became much less vigilant and more in the present when I walked and spent time alone. I saw nature in a new light. I smelled things and saw things much more keenly than ever before. Being mindful: check.

I tattooed a mantra onto my flesh reminding me that *Eunoia* means beautiful thinking, connoting a well-balanced mind. Clarity of thought: check.

I shared my story of abuse and gathered a support group of a few people who would be there for me during the darkest moments and celebrate with me when I made it through those valleys into brighter, more hopeful places. Support people: check!

I journaled and wrote and put my thoughts—good, bad, disturbing, wistful—on paper, leaving a trail from beginning to end. I'd get to the end; there would be a finish line.

I put my healing into a wooden Bridge and platform to symbolize my journey from its start to the hopes of many tomorrows. I left no words unspoken and no thoughts unrecorded. I purged myself of the mental prison I lived in for so many, many years. Freeing myself. Check.

So, why do I keep finding myself back in the spiral of doing well and then falling back into memories, old core beliefs that hinder me from living? Why do I still feel Fear creep up from behind and grab me around the neck, taking my breath away? Why do I sometimes feel like I am four or five and need comfort from another, telling me I'll be okay and that I'm not alone? Why do I get triggered by some things and resort back to cutting and shaming myself? Why?

My therapist reminded me that healing is not a "To-Do" list. There is no special agenda with exercises or remedies that can heal me to a point at which I'm perfect, where my past is my past, and life moves pleasantly forward without pain or memories of painful events.

All the assignments, exercises, and symbols done thus far played a tremendous role in my healing journey. But that's the thing; *it's a journey.* I'm not sure there's an end. I'm learning there are moments when I feel stronger and those moments are lasting longer than in the beginning when I took the first step to get help. I'm learning that even when I feel like Alice in Wonderland falling into a rabbit hole, feeling no ground beneath me, even in those moments, I'm stronger than I was. I have more tools to help me crawl out of that hole and stop spiraling. Sometimes the spiraling doesn't feel like it lasts too long. I catch myself, grab hold, use strategies like self-talk, support people, writing, and spending time with my little girl. That gets me out of that hole pretty quickly.

At other times, I feel like I'm spinning, spiraling into an abyss, and can't make out which way is further down the hole or which way is out, the place where I'm grounded. Those times are lonely, dark, scary, and vulnerable. I don't feel brave and I don't feel healed. I feel isolated and very, very vigilant of all things around me.

But I know this; I hang onto this: I survived sexual abuse for years, so I can survive healing from it. Healing isn't a "To-Do" list. Rather, it is a "To-Do" throughout my lifetime. It doesn't feel fair and it's not because the abuse should never, ever have happened. But. It. Did.

14

Change is Happening

I'm not who I once was. I'm someone who is emerging from a chrysalis, birthing into someone more beautiful, stronger. I'm a woman who believes in the power and determination possessed by all women. I believe women have strength that becomes mightier when we amalgamate that power into positive, life-changing energy. I have that energy. I have that power. I'm learning to embrace it and not to fear it.

I'm a woman with a presence. My voice is heard and my opinions are known. Sometimes my voice is not bridled, for the passion I have takes over my mind and thoughts. I spill them out for all to hear whether to my detriment or not. At times, my thoughts can be used in wise ways, creating change, learning, and more understanding. Other times, when my voice is too critical or falls on deaf ears, it blows like chaff in the wind and is gone.

I have fierce dreams, so fierce, I dare not speak them for how they may sound. I believe I'm gentle and have a depth of understanding about the minds of those around me. I can feel energy and be affected by it. But because of my sensitivity to energy that sometimes makes me vulnerable and I don't like that.

I'm funny and sometimes my humor intimidates others, especially men. Funny women seem to frighten a lot of men. I haven't figured out why, but I do know that when most men experience my sense of humor, they distance themselves from me.

I wear my emotions "on my sleeve," but I don't always express my feelings in healthy ways.

I'm loyal to a fault. When I call you friend or bring you into my world, I trust you and make sure you know you can count on and trust me.

I'm affectionate and believe touch can pass positive energy from one human being to another. I love to stroke a child's face, give them a hug, and make them feel like they are the most special person in the world to me in that moment.

I love exploring new practices like smudging. I love what it means, what it does. I love symbols and creativity. If I could, I'd probably have a symbol for almost everything that matters to me or is significant for my healing.

I try not to hold grudges and see myself as a generally forgiving person, and attempt to focus on the reason why someone wronged me or others close to me, instead of being offended that the person "did that to me."

I love words, meanings of words, how words are used, and learning new words. I love grammar and all the quirky grammar rules that are in our English language. I'm peculiar with things like this but appreciate it as part of what makes me unique (just like everyone else)!

Getting to know myself and feeling comfortable with who I am is becoming easier as I become older. At times, it's still difficult to express self-care, love, and value, but with each layer I heal and each wound I no longer allow to fester, I'm closer and closer to being my authentic self.

15

The Well

When I look back over my life, it seems like I was often sad. Not that I don't have happy memories—I have a lot of them, a lot with my family and friends—but there always seemed to be an underlying sadness deep within my soul.

I smiled a lot, made people laugh a lot, and did crazy, happy things that looked fun and full of excitement or joy. I supposed I did those things for me as well as for others, but I still felt sad in the core of my being. I now know why. I was robbed of innocence in such cold and violent ways. Of course, my little girl was sad! She had a lot to be sad about!

When I connect with the sadness, it's easy for me to go to a place that feels isolated and lonely. A place that feels like I'm going deep within myself with no one else there to comfort me or rescue me. I'm willing to wager that most Survivors can relate to what I call a well of sadness deep enough to swallow us, drown us in our own tears.

I imagine myself by a well. I see a circular stone well with mortar holding its stones together. It's damp to the touch. When I lean over the edge of the well, resting my torso against the cold, hard edge, I look down and see darkness, pitch blackness without end. Sometimes it feels like that's how far my sadness runs—into the depths of the Mariana Trench. The feeling is so endless.

The sadness Survivors feel differs from other kinds of sadness. It's almost indescribable. We can share our stories and heal our wounds, but this sadness sticks to us like crazy glue sticks to something broken. WE are broken. Our little spirits were broken and our bodies were violated. Healing memories, creating tools, and finding strategies that keep thoughts and memories controlled helps the sadness and even brings moments of pure joy and freedom. But this sadness that found itself a home deep within my soul doesn't seem to leave.

Tears release some of the sadness. I strongly believe that when I allow my tears to roll down my cheeks it's to help my heart say the things my voice can't speak, when the bucket at the well has been lowered into that dark hole and is pulled up with water overflowing, spilling from the edges. It's almost as if the bucket has leaks all over and there's no way hands can cover them or keep the water from spilling out. Tears. Those tears are healing tears. They've come from that cold, dark place and found their way out of my soul. They need to come out. My soul needs to experience the grief, the loss that my little one has experienced.

I believe I do okay with my tears. My bucket is lifted frequently from the depth of that place and I weep; I let my tears leak out of me. I let myself be sad, feel sad, and embrace the raw, empty, lonely feelings that accompany it.

What I'm not as good at is letting the bucket empty, drop back down, and come up to release again and again.When I have, it feels like the pressure is so strong my body may collapse from it. I am referring to sobbing, the continuous cry that starts deep within your soul and overflows in ways that your whole body convulses from its pain, its force.

I was afraid I might not survive the "double dipping" of my bucket—that if I embraced the depth of *that* sadness I would never stop crying, and never, ever be okay. But I was. I let my body writhe in the pain, sobbing, crying—letting every vile sound, thought, and experience I had when I was abused and tortured erupt from my very core. I cried. And I cried. Surprisingly to me, but perhaps not to my therapist, I eventually stopped. I was still, quiet, exhausted. The only sound I heard was the little hiccup breaths that follow when visiting the depths in the well of sadness. I survived. I got some of the deep, dark, pitch black sadness out of me. And oh, I felt sad, so terribly, terribly sad.

In my healing, I'm learning about my well of sadness. I'm learning to accept that, in my life, I have a deep well of sadness. Sometimes I dip into it, shed some tears, and then walk away: safe and mobile. At other times, the well beckons me to stay for a while and double dip. It teaches me to go to that place and let some sadness out.

I'm learning it's okay to live with this well, but it doesn't have to dictate my life anymore. I visit the well, but my home is no longer there. In healing, I'm learning that when I am happy, when I am okay, it is okay. I'm learning that my emotions and my memories are not the ruler of this domain. I may have a well of sadness, but I also have a view of the vast ocean of life that lies ahead of me.

16

The Voice

Sometimes I still hear the "Voice." You know, the one that says, "You're crazy! This didn't happen to you. Your family is a good, Christian family that helped the needy, fed the hungry, and gave shelter to the homeless. There is no way this happened." The Voice ends with a resounding, "And NO ONE is going to believe you!"

My heart beats fast in my chest when the Voice speaks. Its fierce claws crawl up from within, trying to suffocate me, trying to rip out my larynx so I will be silent forever. It sounds ridiculous. I know there is nothing in me that can stop the Voice except me. But the Voice is powerful. It's shown its strength and control endlessly through the decades of my life. The Voice has made me believe that if I speak the truth, my abusers will haunt me, hurt me, or even worse, hurt those I love. The Voice has a lot of power over my life.

When I was little and being abused, I knew the Voice had lots of power: frightening, horrific power. Some of the adults in my family were paralyzed in fear from the Voice too. I think I saw that. I believe I determined at a young age that the Voice was stronger than anyone in my family. My grandmother knew. I am certain of it and the Voice silenced her too.

Through my healing, I've come to realize the Voice only has the power silence gives it. When people know about abuse, they can stop the Voice and save the abused. Their power is much stronger than the Voice. The Voice is based on fear of getting caught, being found out, and the victim's shame. When the Voice loses its power, the cycle of abuse shatters like glass dropped onto a concrete floor.

Sometimes the Voice finds its way up my throat and into my mind and I think about what people will say, what people may not believe. But when my Warrior Woman evolves within me, I grab the Voice by *its* throat and crush it with one fist, watching the lies and evil explode from it, obliterated by my power, my truth.

The more Survivors and advocates break the silence, the less the Voice will reverberate in the minds and souls of the abused.

It's not important who listens to my truth. It's important, however, to eradicate the Voice and make it safe for our little children to come forward, to heal, and to be believed. Our courage can move mountains, shake foundations, and stop the Voice once and for all. And when that Voice is silenced, the Survivors' shame and guilt will begin to heal, once and for all, and the shame will transcend onto its rightful owners, the perpetrators themselves.

17

Triggers, Tools, and Strategies

You know that feeling when you're a kid and you lose a tooth? No matter how hard you try to stop it, your tongue goes back to the space where it once was. The voice inside your head reminds you that it's gone—it's no longer there. After a few minutes, your tongue finds its way back to the same place, the empty space where the tooth no longer exists.

I sometimes feel like my memories are like that scenario. I think back to one of my abusive experiences and feel the raw emotion. My mind attempts to tell me I'm okay now, I'm safe. Just like when we first lose a tooth and our tongue goes to that empty place, our memories come back again and again, especially when our healing is just beginning. Like our anatomy adjusts to the missing tooth, our psyche eventually finds ways to cope with and heal memories. Sometimes we dissociate to get through a memory or event. At other times, we might choose a vice to assist us through the pain, the remembering.

I've found as I move through my healing that the memories are not as much of an issue as dealing with triggers and feelings. I believe it's because for so long my feelings were numb; I only allowed myself to go to a certain depth with my emotions in case I couldn't cope. For me, that was part of my survival plan. Now that I experience my feelings much more deeply and authentically, triggers can almost be more terrifying than the memories I used to push back into the darkness.

It's critical in my healing to have tools and strategies ready and prepared so when I'm triggered and my feelings become almost too intense to deal with, I can bring myself back to the moment, remind myself that I'm safe, tell myself to breathe, that it's going to be okay. I've sometimes become physically and mentally aware of my breathing; I slow it down, take deep breaths. I tell myself—usually inaudibly—that I'm safe.

Because I love rituals, symbols, and tactile things, I often resort to other tools and strategies that have helped me focus less on the trigger and more on how to control my thoughts and actions. As I shared earlier, I've a history of cutting. I'm learning that if I don't find a strategy or use a tool during those moments, I will cut. The tools and strategies can be common, shared ideas among Survivors or they can be created uniquely for an individual needing help in times of trouble. One tool is my pen. I also play with molding sand or clay. I either write about or create what I'm feeling. Instead of drowning in my endless depth of feelings, I rescue my soul. I throw myself a life jacket so I can leave the dark, cold, black waters and find a safe place to breathe, to rest.

But we don't create tools and strategies to find ways to forget our past; rather, we create them to help us take control of it. For too long, I used unhealthy tools or strategies, further pushing myself away from self-acceptance and care. Now I'm learning to use my personal tools and strategies to symbolically say "My feelings matter, my thoughts matter, and what happened to me matters." Countless things, sayings, and ideas can be a tool or strategy to help in times of distress.

I was in a grocery store. My mind was leafing through a ton of "working files" and "to-do lists," preparing myself for what to conquer next once I got the groceries. I was okay, doing the grown up thing well, feeling quite stable going through and doing life like every other person that day.

I stopped at the dairy cooler, my mind already moving on to the next thing on the list, when a huge waft of the milk cooler's smell permeated my senses. I might as well have been right back on the farm in the milking parlor. I was triggered. Big time.

My chest tightened, my eyes watered, and I suddenly felt blanketed in fear. I had to get out of there.

I left my cart and almost ran to my car. I got in and clenched the steering wheel as hard as I clenched my teeth. As tears rolled down my cheeks, I wondered what I could do. Then, I remembered. I came back to the present. I remembered I was a woman and not a little child, unsafe, or in danger. I breathed. I said out loud, "You are safe, Pam. No one can hurt you." I took some slower, deep breaths, exhaling loudly. I was grounded again. I got out of the car and walked back to where I abandoned my cart, hoping it was still there or I would have to start all over!

Triggers, tools, and strategies

Triggers seem as inevitable as the memories from our abuse. Tools and strategies are necessary antidotes for the infliction of these situations that literally paralyze us from healing, taking control, and caring for ourselves. My tools and strategies are a work in progress. Sometimes they are easy to use; at other times, I struggle passionately with old habits and coping mechanisms versus new ones. But I'm learning to believe something important: the more I allow myself to reach for the life jacket, the less often I'll feel like I'm drowning.

18

The Sunroom

I often think of my mind as a large house or mansion with different rooms that signify various things in my life. For example, when I'm working hard and doing physical things like cleaning, cooking, laundry, and so on, my mind is in a kitchen. When I write, I often imagine my mind working out of a room with a stone fireplace, wood crackling in the hearth; I'm sitting at a roll-top desk, looking out the window. Snow is gently falling, creating a deep blanket of white on the ground.

Perhaps it's not so much that my mind is like a mansion but rather that I subconsciously visualize places I'm in when doing certain things. In drama classes in university, we were often led through creative visualizations. This was an exercise used to center us, focus us, so we could come into character and tap into our creative senses. Because I've done this exercise many times, it's not awkward or uncomfortable for me when my therapist uses creative visualization in one of our sessions. Let me back up a bit first.

I shared with her that ever since my mother discovered I was writing, I began to feel fear creep up inside of me, paralyzing me. I felt guilty for sharing my story; afraid of hurting people I love with the truth. That Voice that wants to silence Survivors to keep the secrets was raging inside of me.

I told Dr. Mitchell that when I think of myself in that place of fear, I'm in a cold, damp, dark place. I also said that when I feel *my* voice rising and hold *my* truth with confidence, I imagine myself in a beautiful sunroom overlooking a breathtaking view of the sea. I see myself standing tall and strong, confident with choice, my story. I smell the sea air and feel it tickle me ever so slightly across my face, gently blowing sweet promises of energy and love my way.

My therapist wanted me to get back into that room, that place where I'm meant to be and absolutely deserve to be. And so began the creative visualization exercise. Here's my story. This is what I saw, this is what I felt.

Creative Visualization Exercise

The room, if you call it that, is more like a cold, dark hole in the earth: damp and incredibly dark. I was small, with blonde hair and bangs. I sat on a small wooden crate-type box with my body hunched over, hugging my knees. I felt terrified, sad, and completely alone. When I tilted my head up, I could barely see a beam of light, but there was light there. It just seemed far, far away.

I then felt the presence of another person in the dark with me. When I squinted and forced myself to see, I noticed it was adult Pamela. You see, she had come to rescue me, to pick me up and take me out of that place of utter destitution, fear, and sadness.

Before my eyes, Pam suddenly became larger than any human my child had ever seen. She looked powerful and strong, but not frightful. Circling around her was this indescribable pink, cosmic light. It was whirling and swirling with such power and force, but it wasn't scary. It was warm and safe. This pink light, this force of energy, made me feel brave. I found my voice and told Pam that "I really like pink." She smiled at me and I no longer felt afraid.

In some magical, mystical way, I was lifted up by Pam into her strong, caring, and gentle embrace. The pink, cosmic light was now encircling Little Pamela too! With one seemingly easy step, Pam took us out of that hole of fear, that place of sadness. I then was placed carefully beside Pam and I watched as she put a two-by four piece of wood through the door handles, blocking us from entering that place, and barricading anyone or anything from coming out.

It's incredible to me how very real that experience was. I was lost. My little girl was terrified and alone. Then—with confidence, grace, and powerful strength— Pam came and picked me up. She was the Woman Who Picked Up Her Child. The beauty of that thought, the magnitude of what that visualization symbolizes in my healing journey, is almost too powerful to describe. But it happened. I was witness to it. I saw it with my own eyes—but most importantly, experienced it with my entire being.

19

Flashbacks

That visualization came about as a result of the significant and powerful work I was doing with my therapist. Fear has controlled me most of my life. I would either get sucked into it or Fear the Fear of feeling it. When I healed some of my pain by going back to those times when I was abused, I began to experience the memories many times without fear. I relaxed when I was walking, not worrying about who might come along and try to hurt me. I felt safe in my own skin. These moments of confidence were beginning to feel comfortable and, most certainly, welcoming.

Sadly, Fear came-a-knocking at my door once more, paralyzing me and keeping me from writing about my experiences, my journey, and my thoughts. I felt like I had sunk back into a very dark and scary place again because, after doing the creative visualization exercise with my therapist, I experienced a flashback.

When we (meaning my heroine Pam and Little Pamela) left that hole, I suddenly found myself back at the farm, standing by doors at the side of the house. My body was writhing, my throat felt so tight! Every part of my being was ravaged by terrible memories and experiences I had when I was abused. Horrible things happened through those doors. Heinous things. And sadly, I was a victim to them. I cried. I was terrified. I felt like I would be physically sick.

My therapist was there and brought me back to the present. It's a difficult task to come back. It takes courage and strength. The forces and memories love to suck me in like quicksand, a slow and agonizing trap that's impossible to get out of unless there is help. Dr. Mitchell helped me. She reminded me: I'm an adult, that I was in her office and not in that godforsaken place of terror, violence, and abuse. I was dissociating and she brought me back to reality.

It's quite a phenomenon really, when I think of what my small child went through and survived, because when I go through it as an adult—at least the memories of it—I feel like I'm going to die. It's as though Fear attempts to suck me back into its agonizing vortex. I was rescued, and then in the same split second, had violent memories of abuse and torture.

I didn't stay there though. I carried on with the rest of my evening. I was exhausted, quiet, contemplative, and a bit taken aback at the sudden force with which Fear had attacked me again.

It's been three days since that happened. I'm taking each moment at a time. At least, I'm trying to do that. I've resisted self-harm, reminding myself to stay in the moment, that I'm in control. I feel sad sometimes at what adults, not just adults but my relatives, did to me. I feel angry that they got away with it.

I'm attempting to draw from energy and strength beyond me. I'm trying to be aware of my breathing. I'm attempting to take care of me. It's not easy. When my mind lapses back to that place, those memories, I feel so dirty and unlovable that I want to go away and never return. But then....

I think I've come too far for that. Even with the memories, the pain, the triggers, the flashbacks, and the Fear, I'm surviving.

I'm a Survivor! I'm a cosmic force, an energy that deserves to live without darkness and definitely without Fear anymore.

20

New to This Place

I didn't think I had a problem with expressing and embracing my feelings until I began healing my past. Suddenly, this woman who had been told her whole life that she was over-sensitive, a scaredy-cat, dramatic, and moody was now figuring out how to deal with her emotions in a more healthy and concrete way.

When I was a child, I cried a lot. I was extremely sensitive and felt different emotions intensely. For example, I wasn't happy, I was ecstatic. I wasn't afraid, I was terrified. I wasn't quick tempered, I was volatile. It's obvious for me to understand, then, that emotions were not something over which I had control.

Rather, emotions were something that needed to be expressed in a better way.

Although I can't say I've been numb to emotions, it's safe for me to say I never resided in one emotion long enough to experience the authenticity of any emotion except that of fear and sadness—but I've already written about those. In my path to being more whole, I'm experiencing emotions quite new to me; I'm not sure what to do, how to behave. I wonder if it's what an immigrant to a new country feels when they first arrive? They hear conversations but aren't sure what to make of them or how to translate them. Perhaps it's like watching people practice different customs and feeling at a loss to decipher the environment around them.

Lately, I've been finding myself in similar situations with my emotions. I've been with my loved ones and someone may say something that normally wouldn't become an issue. Now, when someone says something that I don't agree with, I feel agitated, frustrated, and uncomfortable in the conversation. Previously, when I disagreed with family or friends, I wouldn't have spoken—or if I had, it would have been in a critical, highly emotional way. I'd have reacted over the top. It takes a lot of self control to measure being authentic against creating small, yet possibly catastrophic situations in social settings.

I'm in a new place. I'm feeling emotions on a different level. I'm on a new road and need to learn how to be true to myself, yet how to respond in appropriate and healthy ways. Ironically, the children I've worked with have a phrase seared into the core of their thinking so whenever I could teach them this, I would: "Feelings aren't right or wrong, good, or bad. They just are. It's what we do with our emotions that matter."

The students were dealing with a lot of anger. My job and passion was to teach them how to feel anger but make healthier choices when they needed to express that emotion. For example, instead of throwing things, take space and walk away. Again, with irony, I feel as though I'm the student needing to learn to regulate my emotions right now.

My partner has seen for years my inability to express myself in healthy ways. In the past, I haven't spoken about my feelings, I haven't expressed my anger. Perhaps on a superficial level but not authentically. Then BOOM! I'd explode with intense anger about something trivial.

At this moment, I'm feeling. Today, I allow adult Pamela to express her feelings and to reside with an emotion that is bubbling up inside. I'm trying to be true to myself and honest with those around me, not going rogue on people but rather experimenting with phrases such as,

"I feel irritated. I'm frustrated. I'm bored with this. I don't want to do that. This makes me feel uncomfortable."

This is a new space for me. I'm learning new patterns. I'm learning to stay with an emotion rather than quickly move from it. The more I heal, the more authentic I become. The more I allow myself to experience the environment around me, the more real I become to myself and to others.This is a new place for me.

Sometimes I feel excited with new experiences. At other times,I pull back, feeling frozen, too exposed and vulnerable.

As I press on, however, being authentic will become familiar to me and even, perhaps, will become my new normal.

21

I Want to Turn Back

Sometimes I just want to go back. Go back to the time when I didn't deal with memories, triggers, and flashbacks. Sometimes I want to be that closed, protected person who doesn't feel everything so deeply or think about things so intensely.

Sometimes I want to go back to a life without mantras, strategies, tools, and support. Sometimes healing feels far more difficult than being protected, vigilant, and hiding from the truth. Sometimes this road to recovery feels like a hamster wheel, always going round and round but never stopping long enough for me to get off.

In the quiet, breathing deeply, I stop and look over the past eighteen months of my healing journey. I take another deep breath in and realize there is no way I've been through and gone through the agony, triumph, pits of darkness, and mountain-top experiences to obliterate all that the work solely to go back to where I was. No. Way.

This kind of thinking and dreaming makes sense to me because for decades that's who I was: afraid, secretive, dishonest with myself and others, sad, and broken. Although that doesn't sound pleasant, that was me and I knew that me. I was also pretty comfortable with that me.

Unfortunately, that me was not there for Little Pamela. She couldn't be. She was far too busy surviving herself. It was impossible to even think about caring for her dear sweet child.

This "healing me work," this new being, is someone I feel like I'm getting to know in new ways. For example, not being afraid has enabled me to take longer walks even in neighborhoods with which I'm unfamiliar. I feel tall, safe, and know I can experience so much more of my surroundings without looking over my shoulder all the time. Little Pamela enjoys the longer walks too. She notices flowers, lavender, bugs, pretty stones, and smiles in the safety of the sun and security of adult Pamela.

It took some time and hard work to get to that place—the place of confidence and security within my surroundings. But I worked through those challenging times. I developed tools and strategies. I learned I'm far more than the horrible abuse that happened to me. I'm the grace that follows.

So, when I find myself wishing I was my old, familiar self, I breathe deeply. I remind myself how far I've traveled across the Bridge and that the rest of my life can be written with the strength and fortitude I've developed through the pain and healing.

This woman, this "new me," is exciting and even sometimes a little frightening to get to know and understand, but she is a Warrior and has wisdom that can help her continue to experience new things instead of wishing to turn back to what once was the familiar.

22

The Woman Who Picked Up Her Child

I've changed. It's hard to explain how, but I've most certainly changed. I feel like a new person inside my own skin. I think I know when this change, this metamorphosis occurred.

I've no doubt in my mind that healing sexual abuse changes a person, any person. So, to say I've changed only now is not quite the truth. I've had many experiences along the way where I've noticed change within myself and some of my perspectives.

I've learned to be more gracious toward myself, more understanding. For example, I no longer feel exasperated when I think of how afraid Little Pamela was growing up. Now I understand why and reassure her by saying (sometimes audibly), "Of course you were afraid. You had every reason to be." That is definitely different; that has changed. I also seem to experience life with less vigilance and caution. I used to think someone was always watching me so I was prepared and kept myself safe by locking doors, closing blinds, and rarely being alone.

Now, I enjoy being alone, rarely draw the blinds, and sometimes leave my door unlocked. Clearly, those are changes in a lot of ways and need to be recognized and celebrated! I truly believe what transformed inside of me on February 18th, 2018—when I did the creative work with Dr.

Mitchell and Adult Pamela rescued Little Pamela—was a monumental change in my healing journey.

Before the guided imagery exercise, I lived most of my life through the eyes of a child who was abused. Because of that, I was afraid more often than not. I functioned as an adult in roles such as partner, parent, colleague, and so on, but the way I responded and perceived things was perhaps more child-like than adult-like.

When I didn't have control, I went into survival mode and did everything within my power to gain that control back. I either cut, dominated, manipulated, or fled situations when I didn't get my way or in which I didn't feel like I had the control. I believe I mostly did these things unconsciously. I didn't see myself as acting like a child for the most part; I saw myself as someone who needed control to feel seen, heard, and safe. I suppose when one is abused, one does not have control; abusers rob our body, heart, mind, and soul, ravaging any form of self there is.

When an adult Survivor senses loss of control, instinct kicks in to do anything to gain back that control. Unfortunately, I sometimes had temper tantrums and sounded far more aggressive than necessary. Yet, at the same time, I was terrified at what lack of control I felt. Just like during the times and events of my abuse.

At other times, in my timidity and insecurities, I approached the world like a child. I was uncertain and anxious, needing approval, praise, and acknowledgment—like a child who is going down a park slide for the first time, needing encouragement and reassurance that it's OK and that someone will be there to catch me at the bottom.

For sure, I covered up that timidity and lack of confidence during different times in my teen and adult life. I over-extended myself and performed and executed many things in positive and excellent ways. I acted both on and off-stage, making sure the reviews were glowing and complimentary for my hard work. I needed to. I needed to stand out so that I could be praised, acknowledged, and reassured that life was okay and that I was okay.

Today, I feel differently. A transformation has taken place deep within the depth of my soul. I no longer "feel" like a timid, anxious, insecure, and "need for control" kind of girl. I've changed. I've come into my adult woman and set up a permanent camp in this place.

On February 18th, 2018, I went to a very dark and deep place, but I went there as a woman. I went there with the sole intent to rescue my little girl from her fear, isolation, and her past. When I went down into that dark place, I saw so vividly and felt a burning within my soul that it was time. It was time to rescue her and bring her home into my loving and capable adult arms. I remember having so much strength when I went to rescue her. I felt larger than life. The cosmic force, the glowing, pink, healing energy light and God around me either would not or could not be penetrated by anything vile that my little girl was experiencing and feeling. I recall stepping down into that hole where she was trapped. There was no physical effort in climbing down to get to her. I was larger than life, with the ability to step down with ease.

The surroundings of that cold, dark, terrifying place didn't spark any fear within me. I didn't flinch; I had one mission and that was to rescue my little girl. Even with the power and strength I had when I picked up my girl child, I felt love and tenderness emanate through every part of my being.

When I stepped out of that horrific and terrifying place that had held my little girl captive for decades, I barricaded the hole with ease and determination so that no one or nothing could go back in or come out. That place was no longer an option of existence, no longer a residence for my dear Little Pamela.

When I embraced sweet Pamela, she clung to me, almost like someone who hasn't seen a loved one and felt danger for them and rushed into their arms with gratitude to find them alive, for they are home safe and sound.

Unfortunately, after the grand rescue and reunion I had in therapy that day, it was immediately followed by the flashback I described in chapter 19. My therapist, in her calm, wise, and gentle way, brought me back to the safety of her office and presence.

When I left that session, I can't recall feeling different per se, but during the following days and weeks, I noticed the transformation within myself, in my thinking and my approach to and outlook on life. I somehow felt more peaceful, confident, and stable, as if a piece of me that had far too much terror and chaos was now silent and calm. I felt more level-headed, assured, and mature in some inexplicable way. The energy around me was different somehow. Within me was a stillness that felt good—not the kind of silence that comes before a storm, but a calm that one may feel sitting quietly in the night under the stars, watching the flames in a fire, listening to the crackling of the wood, seeing the gloaming embers in the pit of the fire.

That experience on February 18th transformed me. I picked up my child and we became one, but instead of her fear and timidity bursting out of me, my woman-self has calmed that part of her spirit with assurance that I now have taken my rightful place of protector and caregiver. This part of my journey brought significant change from how I move in this world, what energy I have within and around me, and how I think about myself and the world around me.

All because I became the Woman Who Picked Up Her Child.

23

Another Test

Great.

One of my molars broke. A piece fell out when I was eating Doritos. It's been more than twenty years since I've gone to a dentist, not for reasons that may be common or obvious. I don't fear the work, the needles, the freezing, or the horrible taste of fluoride. For me, the dental chair takes me to a scary and unsafe place. Growing up and going to the dentist, I must have become an expert in dissociation when I sat in the chair. I probably did that to survive and keep away from the places where thoughts and feelings are taking me today.

That's what healing does, I suppose. As we thaw from our past, become connected to it, look at it, grieve it, and heal it, we are being true to ourselves. We subconsciously state our worthiness to be taken care of, worthiness to be whole.

So, this dental appointment will be another exam in my healing journey. I don't look forward to it. Who looks forward to an exam even if you are prepared for it?

I'm terrified of having tools and equipment inserted into my mouth. I hate the idea of almost lying prostrate with another adult over me who has complete control. Tears immediately well up in my eyes when I think of going. This is definitely a moment in my healing journey where I spiral back into a place of vulnerability and fear.

I'm attempting to use the tools I developed through my journey. I'm trying to strategize and devise a plan so that when I arrive, I will feel safe and in control with my adult Pamela sitting in the chair, not vulnerable, sweet Little Pamela. This is truly an exam!

One strategy is getting a female dentist. That'll help or at least dissipate some anxiety. But it is my darn memories and the feelings that go with the dentist that feel impossible to control!

I have got to do this. My tooth, partially broken, is sharp and cutting my tongue. It's not an option to leave it unless I want something worse to happen or have a sore tongue for the rest of my life. A choice? Yes, but a stupid and uncomfortable one! I feel embarrassed to tell the doctor about my anxiety. If it was because of the "normal" reason, that would be easier. But what does taking care of myself mean? It means advocating for *me*. It means expressing *my* needs and asking others for help around *me*.

Taking care of myself means not being alone and trying to sweat it out only to barely survive. In a written exam, if my pencil breaks, I run out of ink, or I need more paper, I have to ask for help to solve the problem. The proctor or professor will help me. Easy peasy. BUT this flipping exam is a broken tooth not a broken pencil!!!

I'm learning that this path to healing that I'm on has tests and exams along the way. I've yet to decide whether these tests and exams come when I move closer to the end of the bridge—as though it's my abuser's umpteenth attempt to drag me back into their claws of violence and control—or if it's just a natural part of life.

Maybe it's both but, as Survivors, we get the unpleasant task of dealing with the past *and* present. More exams, harder challenges. So, off to the dentist I go.

24

Photo Gallery

The following pages are filled with select photos from my childhood and my healing journey. I include photos from my younger years and a more recent photo; examples of the healing exercises with clay; my healing Bridge; playing with pebbles; pebble art; and Shea, my beloved companion on my healing journey.

Photo 1: Four-year old Pamela.

Photo 2: Nine-year old Pamela.

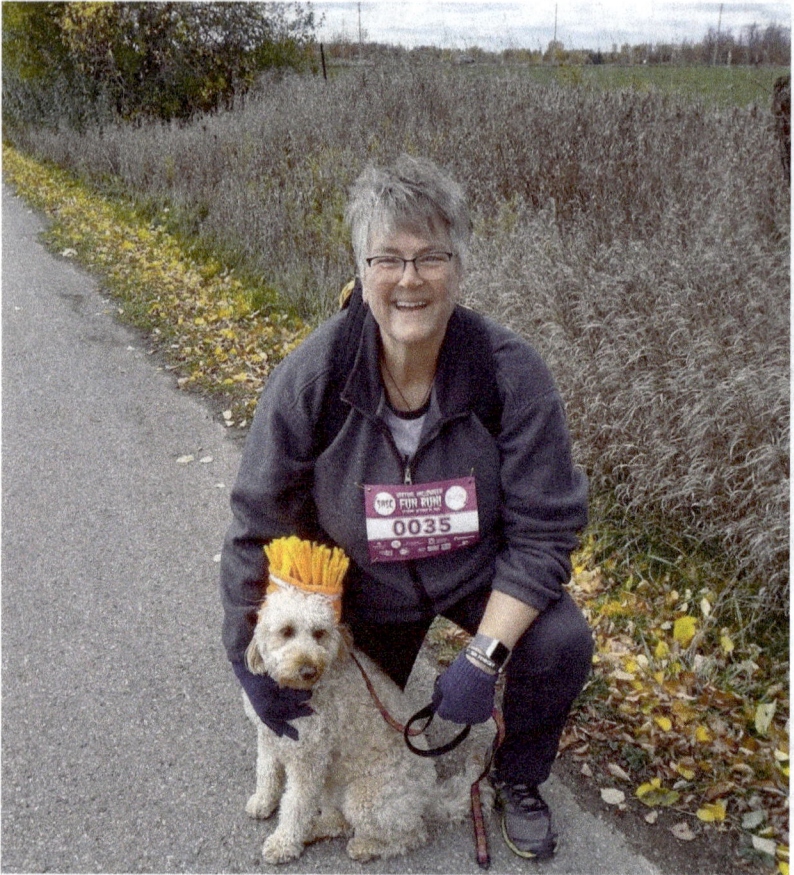

Photo 3: Pamela, age fifty-two, with Sadie, my current dog.

Photo 4: The well of sadness, to remind me that it's a place to go but not to stay.

Photo 5: Exercise in molding sand: using shells as a vehicle for healing.

Photo 6 (top): The complete Bridge. Photo 7 (bottom): The door to the Bridge, with Little Pamela and Pam at the entrance to my healing Bridge.

Photo 8: The stairs to the Bridge.

Photo 9: The screen door from the Bridge to the platform; I can LOOK back at my past, but I don't need to GO to my past.

Photo 10: *The platform at the end of the Bridge represents the beginning of the rest of my life.*

Photo 11: Railroad tracks on the platform at the end of the Bridge remind me there are different options.

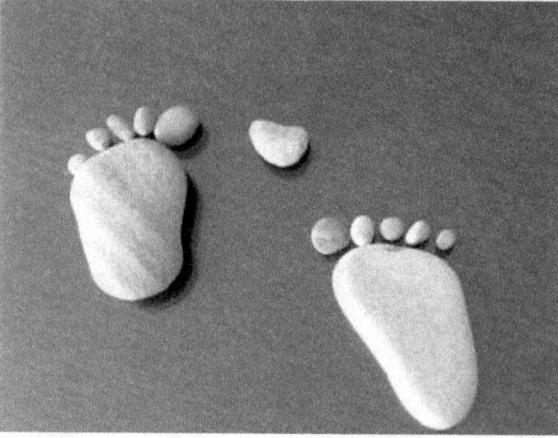

Photo 12 (top): On the beach, "HOPE," a healing exercise with pebbles.
Photo 13 (bottom): Playing with pebbles from the beach.

Photo 14: The day I chose "LIFE" at the beach.

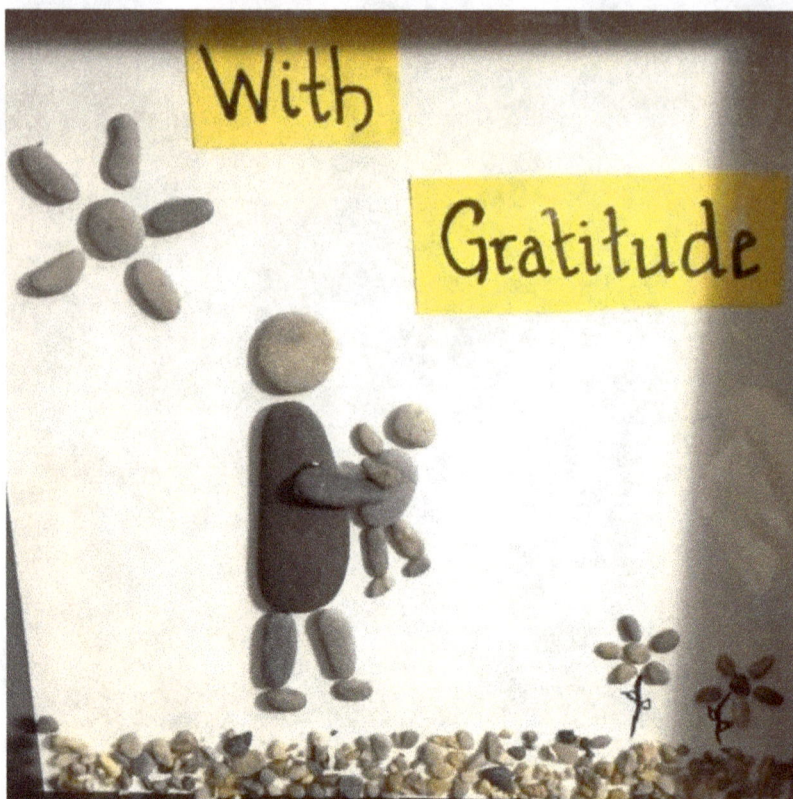

Photo 15: The Woman Who Picked Up Her Child.

Photo 16: Playing with my child through pebble art.

Photo 17: Sharing my pebble art at a local craft store.

Photo 18: Shea, who traveled with me on my healing journey.

25

The Journey to the Dentist

The hardest part in getting to the dentist is asking for help along the way. Putting the address into my phone is easy. I got the directions without issue; I wasn't concerned about getting lost or not finding the office in time. However, I've yet to find an app on my phone that directs me through the process of dealing with the fear and trepidation that going to my appointment gives me. I needed help.

I emailed my therapist after sharing the truth to my partner about not going to the dentist for over twenty years. I tried to receive her love and care instead of shrugging it off, which once again made Little Pamela feel like her pain and fears embarrass me.

In the email to my therapist, I asked for help. She was the one who gave me the name of a female dentist. I called the dentist's office, but immediately—because of what is happening in my psyche—I joked with the receptionist about how long it had been since my last dental visit and commented on how breaking a tooth is one way to stop eating Doritos!

I didn't honor Little Pamela's feelings, but I did make an appointment. And then, I thought about IT almost continuously. Talking about IT with my partner resulted in shallow breathing and tears. But I knew I needed to get my broken tooth fixed...somehow.

I reached out to my dear Survivor friend, Barbra. She acknowledged my fears but reminded me it's Adult Pamela's responsibility to take of and advocate for Little Pamela. When I told her I would feel like my dirty laundry would walk in to the dental office ahead of me—and that's what they would see and think about when they are with me—Barbra said that perhaps Little Pamela is tired of being seen as dirty laundry and that I need to let go of the belief that the shame is mine to carry instead of my abusers'.

What happened next surprised me.

I felt anger that Little Pamela was referred to as dirty laundry—even though they were my words and Barbra was just referring to something I had already alluded to. I was so angry. I almost stopped communicating with her, but what she said actually helped. Having that image of Little Pamela thinking I see her as dirty laundry, and being embarrassed by her, made me get back to my rightful beautiful, brave, amazing, and protective adult self, and advocate for Little Pamela about her anxiety concerning the dentist.

So, I was challenged to write an email that let the dentist know a little bit about my past so she could understand why I would be anxious and afraid.

I wrote it, but there was no email for the dental office. On to Plan B: Tell the dentist when I arrived at the office on the day of my appointment. In the meantime, my partner was here for me to share my feelings or thoughts. It was on my mind a lot, but I used the strategies of self-talk and reassurance whenever my thoughts attempted to take me to dark places.

The day of the appointment arrived. I was anxious but also wanted to get there and face my fears. I kissed my partner and went on my way. The receptionist was so kind and friendly. When it came time to share about my childhood sexual abuse and torture, I knew I could because she made me feel comfortable and safe.

I also had the opportunity to speak with my dentist privately. She was receptive to me telling her about my history and said she was sorry it had happened but assured me that I'm not alone and then asked what would help me cope while I'm there. And I did it. I advocated for myself! My voice was cracking and my eyes had tears, but I spoke. I told her I needed to be told what she was going to do before doing it. I needed to see the tools before she used them and I needed her to tell me what they were.

I wish I could say I magically went through the entire tooth repair not having one flashback or memory, but I didn't. I can say I managed myself well, though, and dealt with my thoughts without the knowledge of anyone around...except if they had looked at my hands. I was squeezing them mercilessly and definitely "white-knuckling" it.

When it was quiet and my thoughts slipped away, I needed to bring myself back to the present. I became aware of my breathing. I found and named (silently) five things around me. When the hygienist and dentist spoke with one another, I listened to them acutely and made a concerted effort to keep myself in the present, assuring Little Pamela that I, the adult, have this situation under control and I'm taking care of her. For example, when my chair was being raised, I instantly pictured Little Pamela being lifted onto that dirty table in the shed. I felt tears well in my eyes. I took deep breaths. I looked at my legs, my adult legs, and told myself, "I am grown. I am present." I crossed my legs and clutched my hands tighter. I didn't feel badly about myself because I was protecting my little girl.

A little over an hour passed and I was finished. My tooth was fixed and I was thanking them for their kindness and sensitivity. Another exam conquered! I did not sign up for this class, but I did sign up to heal. Tests, midterms, and exams happen throughout this course I call healing. With pride and victory, I can actually, authentically, say, "I nailed this exam!!! I am going to celebrate! My Little Pamela is getting an ice cream sundae" —oh, as soon as her mouth unfreezes...

26

Healing Uniquely

We all heal differently. We recall different memories. We take longer at some points in our healing than at others along the journey of setting ourselves free from the past horrors of childhood sexual abuse. We create our own maps when we heal.

One important piece in creating my own map of healing is to remember I'm already free. My therapist asked me to look at going through this differently than serving a life sentence from what my abusers did. She asked me to look at it as though I had lived a life sentence but NOW I was free. She challenged me to look at my life as someone who WAS in prison but has NOW been released. Just like a released prisoner, I have to learn how to live in freedom.

As soon as we disclose our abuse to someone, anyone, we've unlocked the door to our prison. The map is now in our hands. Our job—in this case, my job—is to get out of my cell and walk out of the prison completely. This is where hard work begins. Even though I can see the opening to my cell and even though I can physically leave, it is excruciatingly difficult to do so.

Please understand that when any of us discloses our abuse, it takes incredible courage and bravery. It takes trust, and most Survivors don't have an abundance of trust in the first place. So, unlocking the cell door is an incredible task in and of itself. It will take some of us years to walk out of this prison. Others, perhaps not quite as long. The point is that freedom is ours for whenever we choose to go after it, remembering that the map for each path differs for each Survivor. It's like we're part of the same storm but each has a different type of boat to navigate through the waves.

For me, years passed as I stood and looked at the opened door but didn't walk through it. I suppose I felt less afraid of my prison cell than I did in creating and working on a map that could help me to be free. I was more comfortable with pushing memories away and trying to forget the abuse. In my twenties, I did some good work around my abuse, but somehow ended up back in my prison cell. I guess I felt way more comfortable with my own space, my own thoughts, thinking I was safer there than going through the cell door. I felt like I knew my surroundings far better in my own prison than the freedom and open space beyond my familiar thoughts, memories, and coping skills.

When I felt I could trust my supporters, especially my therapist, I eventually stepped through that door. I imagine that a prisoner who has served her time walks quickly to the exit that sets her free. I did not. I spent months lingering at the cell door. Some days, I think I even could have been seen as a loiterer.

First, I want to talk about my lingering. Although I had trust in my partner, therapist, and a few close friends, I didn't trust myself with this new potential of freedom. So, I stood by the cell door, ready to step back into the familiarity and comfort even if it was painful and my thoughts claustrophobic at times. I knew how to deal with that; I'd learned how to survive.

When lingering at the door, I sometimes took a few steps forward, working on ways that better helped me deal with the future, my future, that which was ahead of me. In those steps, I learned to accept new ways of thinking and coping. I tried out some strategies that became tools to use when triggered by a memory from prison. During those times, I let go of the cell door and took a few steps. Even if I circled back to my cell, I'd taken more steps toward freedom than ever before.

Loitering was a different experience for me. When I'd built the trust, developed strategies, and had tools handy in case of emergencies, I consciously didn't want to leave. Prison had been my home. What if I would never see it again?

What if walking away made me become someone completely unrecognizable? What if I would have a voice, experience success, feel confident? What if others would notice the change and see me differently? What if I would see myself differently? So, I loitered. Leaning against the open cell door, I felt like I was okay not going back in but certainly not okay to step out into space that was wide open for me.

"What ifs" can keep us cemented in time where we become frozen, not living in the past, not living in the present, and certainly not looking to the future in a positive light. The "what ifs" are a gang of thoughts that keep us from moving forward. They seem to be okay in not letting us go backward, but certainly want us to remain where we are, trapped in fear, by controlling our thoughts to capture us and keep us from forging ahead.

Lingering and loitering are coping mechanisms. In my case, they sometimes keep me breathing. The reality is that, in prison, one often needs to be with a gang to feel protected and safe.

I wish I could say the hall I needed to walk through to find the EXIT door to my new lease with freedom was a short journey. It took me years! But that's normal in comparison to sentences given to inmates for their crimes. I feel thankful I eventually did push the door open and walk into freedom, my freedom. It took a lot of love and trust from my supporters. It took courage I didn't know I had.

Sometimes in my journey to freedom, I find myself running back to the door from where I came. I find myself banging on it, hoping someone will let me back in! I cry, sometimes scream, to have that door opened so I can run back to my cell and curl up on my cot in a fetal position, eyes closed, allowing all the horrible fear and memories to latch onto my brain once again. Because that, however horrible, feels safer than the new feelings and experiences.

But then, with all the strength I can conjure up inside, I allow myself to think about how far I've come, how hard I've worked, how long my undeserved sentence has already been. My therapist gently reminds me: my freedom puts shame on its rightful owners. My abusers no longer have power or control.

I do.

Freedom is changing me. How could it not? When I think of prisoners who lived most of their lives in a cell and were then released, the profound effect freedom has is enormous. Sometimes freedom is too much for me to imagine to move toward and I choose to stay in my cell, hoping the fear and memories don't consume me but rather, in some warped way, bring comfort.

Sometimes, the "what ifs" swallow me and I lose the battle, closing the door and allowing darkness to swallow me. But, for the times when I choose freedom, to bravely walk toward it and triumphantly claim it as my own, the results are far more than I believe I can even consciously grasp or fathom.

I often thought of remaining a prisoner. I often thought of letting the gang of "what ifs" take me forever into its clutches, but I didn't. And if you are reading this, neither did you.

Healing is different for each of us. Our maps and our journeys are all unique.

Regardless, they lead us to freedom. The journey's terrain isn't easy.

It's rugged terrain, with dense forests and valleys. However, I also see waterfalls, beautiful views that stretch out endlessly, and the great gift of possibilities before us. I must say, I'm liking freedom more than my cell.

I'm different. Sometimes people notice, sometimes not. Either way, this difference in me is not harmful, just freer, more strongly grounded. I'm also loving my voice: it's confident and self-assured. My voice hopefully helps others in their journey to freedom. My voice helps me to stand up for my little girl who, decades ago, lost hers to her abusers. I'm gaining authentic confidence and learning to see myself as a much stronger, capable woman.

It takes time to heal and I'm not blind to the fact that I'll find myself pounding on the prison's door again. But I do know this and I believe this: each time I go back, I cry for a shorter time, my screams don't last as long, and I stop pounding on the door in a shorter amount of time than the last time I was there. I center myself. I look at my map and see how far I've come with Freedom as my goal and begin trekking back to where I was with Hope as my compass and Courage as my guide. We all deserve this freedom. We all deserve this gift to give ourselves over and over as many times as we need.

27

Spirals

I've decided I hate spirals. I hate what they do, symbolize, and mean—at least within the realm of healing. I feel like I'm going along, doing okay, handling the bumps and curve balls that life usually throws my way. Although sometimes the situations are more difficult than others, I'm handling things relatively well. I determine this by not having self-harmed or gone down dark corridors in my mind that eventually take me to suicidal thoughts and plans. I've sometimes even talked to others about my feelings. Avoiding these things and using tools and strategies are choices worth celebrating.

Then suddenly, BAM! Out of the blue, a trigger, memory, or feeling comes rushing into my mind and body seemingly out of nowhere and I'm thrown back into a spiral! I no longer feel like I can or want to climb back up. I wind through the paths, searching for, recalling, and using tools and strategies to help get me back to where and when things were okay and sometimes even good.

I tire of three steps forward, two steps back. Enough already! I look at others and do the deadly deed of comparing my life to theirs. They are skipping along their journey with ease and grace.They smile and succeed at what seems like all they do.

Then there is me. I can't even find my way out of a spiral!

Lately, such dark thoughts cloud my mind again. I want to and think about cutting all day. Then I think about just taking my life once and for all. Ending the fight. Saying to myself, "They win! I gave it a good shot, had some great moments of freedom but, it's over. I just can't do it anymore."

You know why? I don't know where to get the energy to climb back out. It's like I'm sitting on a ledge in the spiral. My little girl is cuddled tight into my side; my arms are wrapped around her tired little body. I see her wet bangs pasted to her forehead from the pure sweat of our journey together. I can tell she's so tired of falling and climbing, searching, and fighting.

I feel my own sweat trickle down my neck and sense fatigue in the very core of my soul. I'm an adult and I can't even muster up the strength to pick myself up and look to the light, reach for it, and climb toward it.

I'm at this place again: the place where I want to just fade away into people's memories and become part of the past. That place feels quiet, peaceful. My mind and body grasp for the stillness; the absence of triggers, memories, and sadness; the complete void of thoughts, fighting, battling, or movement of any kind.

I glance into the mirror and see my sad, teary eyes looking back at me. They appear empty, yet pleading for something, anything. Sometimes I choose not to self-harm and not to end my life because of my daughter. I remember someone saying to me that any reason to not take your life is okay. If we can't choose life because we want it or feel worthy, at least we stay alive for someone or something.

Right now, I'm writing and living because of her. Perhaps that's all I need for now. Perhaps I need to just rest in that knowledge. I certainly don't feel like using strategies or tools to help me out of this spiral. My little girl and I don't have the energy.

I can only imagine rock climbers and how they must be completely exhausted yet have to keep going: find the right crevice to perch one's foot on, search for a crack with enough ledge that one can grip onto, hoist themselves up...only to start all over again! I bet not many Survivors rock climb. It's too much of what we do mentally all the time!

I'm thankful for those who helped along the way: my partner and her endless support and love; my therapist and her support, wisdom, and belief in me; my dear friend Barbra and her understanding and encouragement through it all; my sisters and brothers who have patiently walked parts of this journey with me. For them, I am forever grateful.

Today, I stay on that ledge in the spiral, too tired and exhausted to move, emotionally drained and mentally devoid of any will to keep on keeping on. I waiver with the thought of staying on this earth, this way, even for my daughter Danikka. I see her as a strong, resilient woman who is a fighting Survivor herself with so much to offer and give to this world. Me, not so much.

Tears roll down my face as I write these words because I wonder where the Warrior Woman has gone. Has she left forever, giving up on me because too many times I've fallen back into this spiral of darkness and death? It wouldn't surprise me, because here I am again on the edge, contemplating the will to move or make the decision to say, "Enough!"

I have to say, in this moment, right now, as I write this, it is a draw. It is so depleting, exhausting. At the end of the day, I fall into bed thinking, "What will be different tomorrow?" I wish I had answers, that somebody did, but I don't think this is going to change with magical words.

It's only going to change when the shame of the abuse that happened to me is completely purged from me and placed onto its rightful owners, the abusers themselves. It will change if I believe I deserve freedom, success, and happiness. It will change if I stick with my little girl and whisper, "We can do this. Just hold onto me. I got you and I won't let you go."

28

Full of Depletion

To be full of something that is reduced seems like an oxymoron, but that's how I feel, or at least how I felt until I knew I had to provide myself with care: whole, kind, gentle, and unwavering self-care.

Healing from the devastation and repercussions from childhood sexual abuse is a full-time job. But, like any process I've gone through—whether grieving or changing—life continues on around me. That's exactly what's happened on this journey of healing.

Many things in my life seemed to happen as I was healing, moving forward, and writing my own story. For example, several things at work happened that felt hurtful, mean, deliberate, and unpredictable. I was devastated; a lot of wind left my sail. And that only seemed to be a small part of what I needed to deal with.

My partner was in a terrible motor vehicle accident and, as a result, needed hospitalization and rehab for four months. I was left to deal with countless tasks on my own, including the things happening at work. My energy was slowly leaving me like a balloon that, over time, loses air ever so slowly. I kept working on my inner healing, trying to put my needs first when I could, but life got in the way.

After six months of agony at work and stress at home, I felt full, full of Depletion, that is. Everything seemed and was overwhelming. The things I enjoyed doing, like walking my dog, felt like it took energy I no longer had. I completed essential household duties and sometimes not even that. Laundry piled up until I needed to do it—unless I wanted to live in a nudist colony! I scrounged around for food and only went shopping when the cereal box was empty and the milk carton in recycling. Indeed, I was becoming a glutton of Depletion.

When this happens to me, my life becomes dark. I become cynical and walk into the shadows where that inner voice calls my name, questioning my desire to live and for what reason. I can quite easily go there, to that place where death is more inviting than life. I imagine taking myself, full of Depletion, and ending it all. This time I even have a plan. I gave some possessions away and got rid of "junk" so that others didn't need to be bothered with it after my death.

The emptiness was so deep. I couldn't see light when I looked up. Below me was dark as pitch. I looked ahead and saw countless responsibilities; behind me was worse. I couldn't see how far I'd come. I could only see the pain, the sadness, and the seemingly endless effort in my life—and for what? So that I could be filled with Depletion, so that I'd come to this place again? I'd ask myself how living could possibly be worth it when all I felt was total emptiness and saw only black. It felt impossible. I knew I needed help.

In my healing journey, I've needed and still need to learn to ask for help. I'm still learning to not walk this journey alone. That's incredibly difficult for me. I think it is for most Survivors. For so long, I learned to keep my thoughts and feelings inside. As a child, it probably kept me alive, but as an adult I think it's caused more pain and harm than anything else. And to me? To me it brings inner turmoil, isolation, and the desire to knock on death's door.

I was full: full of emptiness, full of Depletion. I needed to listen to those two people I reached out to. First, my therapist helped me see that I desperately needed to do some self-care. My partner helped me execute a plan for exactly that.

It was difficult to not feel selfish and greedy for requesting time to myself for myself. Somehow, being full of emptiness led me to take that Depletion seriously and begin a crucial step in learning the importance of emergency self-care.

29

The Importance of Self-Care

Finally, the day arrived. I wasn't sure if I would make it to this day, nor was I sure my little "retreat" would happen. But I woke up, packed, and the time actually came for me to leave. Well, for us to leave. I took my dog Shea with me for some quiet company.

I arrived at my destination shortly after check-in. I smiled to myself when the woman at the front desk started typing the bill into the Interac machine as I held cash out to her. It's like she hadn't seen money in a long time and wasn't sure what to do with it; she had to call her manager to help her find the cash box. A small giggle bubbled out of me. I felt relaxed for the first time in a very long time. I was present and living in the moment.

Shea and I found our cabin. I could hear the waves washing onto the shore from my temporary new home. I could smell fresh air and was aware of all my senses. I could see the fresh colors of spring all around me and, as I turned the key into the lock to open my cabin door, was aware that even that felt adventurous and exciting! After I unpacked, it was time to explore my outdoor surroundings. I immediately walked to the beach and, for the first time in countless days, I felt Depletion leave my soul and little gushes of hope move into residence instead. I was taking care of me with my little girl once again in my arms.

With my dog beside me, I gazed out over the vastness of the lake and took in the colors, the air, and the beauty of every direction. I stretched out my arms, threw my head back, and smiled. I knew I'd left death's door. I knew because my breath was deeper, stronger. I knew because my little child was close by my side once again.

Down on the pebble beach, I happily looked for stones to spell *hope* in the sand. I spent the time I needed looking at that powerful word, then I left it there, just like the times I left shells in different places in my neighborhood. For those needing a small gift of beauty, my desire is that whoever finds my word made in stone will see it and feel it, but mostly own it.

I climbed back up the ninety-eight stairs to my cabin with Shea in my arms so her paws wouldn't slip between the wide spaces between the metal stairs. A cardio workout for sure!

I made one of my favorite meals; when it was ready to eat, I took in the soft lapping sound of waves splashing onto the beach. As I got ready for my first night in the cabin, I took Shea out to do her last pee. As soon as the door latch clicked into place, I realized I'd left the key on the table. . Both doors were locked. The lodge was empty. I was the only one around. It was 9:00 p.m.

In the past, being alone in a place like this would have been a nightmare. Being locked outside and having to problem solve would have caused sheer terror to come flooding over me, drowning me with despair. This time, I felt no fear. Sure, I saw a problem, but I felt no fear. That was huge! I didn't have a leash, I didn't have my phone, and it started to rain.

I didn't know whether I should laugh or cry! I definitely saw the humor in it, but I also had no idea if anyone was around to help me. I walked across the road with Shea in my arms, hoping to find someone.

The door to the front desk was locked. The door to the restaurant was locked. When I peered in through the darkened window, all was black except for the lights on the beer taps. I could've used a drink right then! I started to think of places Shea and I could sleep outside. My car was locked—those keys were beside the door key in the cabin. I started to feel desperate. As I walked around the building, it started raining harder. I found an unlocked door and went inside, planning to sleep in the hall if all else failed.

I peered down a corridor and was startled to see the manager of the lodge walking toward me She was surprised to see me in the motel area, quite a way from my cabin, holding a wet dog, and looking pretty soggy myself! I explained my predicament and, within minutes, my problem was solved and Shea and I were cuddled up in the cabin getting warm by the fireplace.

I took care of myself. I took care of my little child. I didn't panic and let fear consume me. In fact, I was thinking more about the humor of paying to sleep outside! I saw it as an adventure. I solved the problem. The sound of the waves lulled me into a deep sleep.

Self-care comes in all forms. I'm learning I first need to take the time for me. When I do that, I can feel hope, see life as an adventure, and embrace it instead of running from it in fear.

30

Playing on the Beach

It's so important to have fun and to enjoy what I'm doing, but when I'm full of Depletion, fun is the last thing I want to do or think about. It takes too much energy—energy I don't have. However, the next morning, the rising sun slowly burned the mist off the surface of the lake and waves rolled languidly onto the beach. I knew: it was time to play.

A wonderful thing about Lake Huron is that the beaches are full of stones and pebbles: a perfect combination of fun. I collected pebbles and stones of different shapes and sizes, thinking about how smooth and round some of them are. How long has it taken them to get this smooth, beautiful, and sparkly in the sun? My healing is like that of a stone in some ways. I need numerous, countless waves of healing to smooth out the pain, to wash away the sadness so I can sparkle. It takes time; I must remember that. I also must remember that, in the meantime, I can have fun and play in the sand with the stones, creating whatever I want!

I jammed my pockets full of the stones I thought I might need and got to work playing. It was so fun! The breeze gently blew in my hair, the warmth of the sun softly kissed my skin, the sound of the waves whispered in my ears, and the texture of sand beneath my feet squished out shoe prints with each step; I began creating pictures of how I felt... and I felt wonder-FULL. I made flowers, sunshine, words, and a picture of my little girl and I running on the beach with balloons! The day was glorious!

When I look back at my childhood, I see moments where I needed care, tender care, and for many reasons I understand now, I didn't receive what my little spirit needed. I think I'm not used to getting what I need so I don't try. It's more familiar to live in sadness looking at others with what they have, forgetting I can have joy and fun too.

I'm learning, slowly. I'm learning I'm not a child any longer and, as an adult, I can create my life, choose things, make things happen. Even as I write this, it bewilders me. I've been an adult for a long time. Why has it taken me decades to grow up? In my mind's eye, I see my little girl and a wave of compassion floods over me. I gently tell myself there are reasons: many, many reasons.

Through my healing, I've grown up somehow. I think when I embraced all the horrendous and painful abuse I survived, I grew up. Now, in my grown-up mind, I'm learning to truly be the author of my life. I can do what I want. I can play in the sand, make pebbles, laugh at the wonder I see in my dog as she tries to figure out the waves splashing onto the shore. I can smile when I think of being locked out of my cabin in the rain. I'm an adult. I can play, enjoy the moment, and take care of myself. It's a wonderful gift, one to embrace far more often than I do.

31

When Self-Care Comes to an End

Does it? I mean, does it really have to come to an end? I think the answer is yes and no. To go away to the lake for three days to do exactly what I want, when I want, is the epitome of self-care. It was nothing short of exactly what I needed.

Unfortunately for me, it was only a small break in my reality and, sooner or later, it was going to have to end. I wished I could have bottled the sound of the lake, the smell in the air, the sights around me, and the serenity I felt walking in the bush or by the lake. Instead, I filled a container with pebbles and stones to make awesome sorts of memory art at home. Reality will come quickly when I get home. My job will become that of caregiver, taxi driver, daughter, and mother; too soon these three days will become a memory. Oh, but the memories will be divine!

I want to remember this time as a crucial and vital part of my healing and living. I want to hold it close, tattooed onto my brain, so I can remember the importance of taking care of me: doing special, separate things, for me.

I waited too long. I take most of the responsibility for that. Next time I feel depleted, I need to take care of myself as soon as possible, not when I'm already empty and so depleted I'm too tired to continue. I want to learn to take good care of myself: to see myself as worthy and significant and important enough to care for.

This time was a gift to me and for me. I can't always do things like this, but I can do small things regularly to remind me to take care of myself. I survived my past; now I want to embrace my future in a worthy and caring adult way.

32

Breath

My breath is the closest thing to me. It's inside me. Even when it leaves my lungs, it's still the closest thing to my being. It can be short and quick, long and slow, but while I am living, it's always here.

Unless my breath changes from its norm, I rarely think of it. It's just a part of me like my hands, body, face, or feet. When I exert myself, I'm very aware of my breath. When I'm struggling with a chest cold, I'm also very aware of my breath but, for the most part, I don't think about my breath.

I'm aware of others' breath more quickly than my own. Certain breath—like onion or garlic breath—is more pungent to smell than other breath. When someone else is wheezing or short-winded, I notice their breath, their breathing, but my breath is just my breath.

That's why I'm sometimes amazed at the sheer power breathing and our breath have. Of course, breathing and breath are necessary for us to live, but beyond that, it holds great power.

I'm often triggered by a memory from my past by breath changes: it's quicker, with short inhales and faster exhales. It seems to be trying to "catch up" with my mind as though the two are racing against each other.

My breath changes when I cry. It gets lodged in my throat, stuck there like sludge in a drain, blocking the pipes. I have to be reminded to breathe, to let my breath out, to let my breath take my sadness with it as it leaves my body. Like memories, breath can get stuck inside of me and then, when my mind and body are ready to release the emotions of those memories, my breath becomes trapped inside me. However, I'm learning through my breath that the closest air to me has become my teacher, my closest ally at times.

It's not been easy to learn this art of controlled breathing: to allow my breath to conquer my emotions and slow my thinking down to a more bearable and capable state. Like most things, I need to practice and know my breath. It's ironic that the very first, natural thing I did out of my mother's womb was to breathe, to accept breath from my new surroundings. Yet now, through my healing, I'm learning again about the power of this life-giving force we call breath.

For me, it's difficult to breathe, to welcome breath, when I'm sad or when I'm hurt or even when I'm angry. When I'm sad, it stays stuck in my throat and I need to remind myself to let that breath out with the sadness that, at times, seems cemented to the inside of me. When I'm physically hurt, I immediately hold my breath, capturing all the pain inside my body trying to just "get through it." Although it's probably a strategy I learned to use to survive my abuse and torture, it's neither a healthy nor necessary strategy to use now.

I've had enough physical pain both in child and adulthood that I no longer need to hold onto and harbor the pain inside me, past or present. I'm practicing even with small pain like stubbing my toe. I'm telling myself to breathe, to be aware of my breath. It's usually pretty sloppy: it comes out sounding like grunts or pants like I'm trying to get through a contraction or something!

By practicing and doing this, I'm helping Little Pamela heal. I believe I'm unconsciously telling her, through my breath, that it's okay to let the sadness and pain go. I'm telling her we no longer need to hold onto emotions; we no longer have to hold our breath to survive the present. I'm taking care of her with my breath, the closest thing to both of us.

The most difficult challenge for me recently is managing my breath through anger. First of all, anger is not an emotion I readily share. When I have, it's not expressed in healthy ways most of the time. I hang on to my anger and I'm starting to think that I have more than I ever thought I did. I'm angry at my abusers, angry that I wasn't protected, angry that they got away with it, and angry that it's a part of who I am yesterday, today, and every day that I have breath.

I've learned to push my anger down so deeply inside of me and seal it with my breath, telling myself, "Shhhh! Don't let it out!" It festers inside me and that doesn't make my little girl feel safe. It makes us both feel afraid, irrationally afraid, and then we don't breathe but rather use our breath to push it further and further out of mind.

I've been told I'm good at exploding with anger. I suppose it's because there's a lot of it to be expressed. I usually have an "over the top" reaction that doesn't help the situation. I've noticed my breath changes when I'm angry, too. I clench my teeth to try and stop the anger from exiting my body, my mouth. I know I'm trying to control the depth of my anger by keeping it inside, so I keep my teeth clenched together to protect those I love. In doing so, I'm not taking care of Little Pamela, nor am I taking care of grown-up Pamela. I am putting others first, protecting them and giving up breath, putting my needs last.

My therapist did an exercise with me around breathing: take a deep breath, then a couple of little ones to expand my lungs to their full capacity. She asked me to then hold my breath for a few seconds—I'm good at that—and then, with as much force as possible, using my entire being, force out the air quickly and powerfully. It was strange. I felt strange, awkward, self-conscious. But again, she nailed what I need for Little Pamela in my past and what I need in the present, right now. I have an anger inside of me that Little Pamela needs to release. Through this forceful, awkward, catch-and-release breathing, my anger could dissipate through breath. I need to tell myself over and over again: my breath is a powerful tool to add to my repertoire for healing my wounded soul.

It's going to take time with breath, breathing. I'm learning to befriend my breath, to accept her strength and power. I'm trying to learn that with every breath, every exhale, I can let go of sad pain and anger and keep the goodness that makes me the Warrior Woman I am—at least, for today.

33

The Feelings, the Pain

Images of my little girl flood my mind. I go back to that dark place again. I see her sad, little face; I recall every piece of clothing she is wearing and I remember. I can physically feel the pain in her body. Now, decades later, it envelops me. The pain intensifies and literally takes my breath away.

In my adult body, I begin to writhe with the pain I felt when I was violated. I hold my breath because I can't bear to take in this tremendous assault. My stomach hurts. My body feels like it's breaking apart, inside and out. I want to evaporate; if I hold my breath long enough, maybe I will. That's what I think now. I imagine I did many years ago too.

I can't get out of the pain. My mind is reeling; I am filled with the savage beast of Fear again. It ravages my body. The terror of the beast has robbed me of my breath. Yet again, I'm in the grips of Fear's horror, being strangled from all good things and swallowed into the pitch black of abuse and pain. I see my little girl after another devastating encounter with my abuser. I feel him. I can taste him. I'm smothered by his ravenous body of hate and atrocities. What did I do? What did my little girl do to have this evil done to her?

I'm in the aftermath of what just happened. My present body is floating above where my little girl sits. She's on the lap of my older cousin. Our eyes meet. I feel her pain too. I look deeply into her blue eyes and I see a depth of sadness that seems to have no end.

In the distance, I hear a faint voice. It's my therapist. She's trying to bring me back, back to her room, back to the present. I can hear her, but I can't seem to move or "come back." I feel paralyzed, morphed into my past. My eyes are locked onto my little girl child. Dr. Mitchell beckons me to come back to the present. I feel devastated. Another memory. Another plunge into the place where fear, pain, and sadness devour me.

For a split second, I come back and look into the eyes of my therapist. I'm safe. I'm not at or near the farm or those perverted beasts. I'm encouraged to pick up my little girl, to hold her, and remind her that it's over. We are safe, with a safe woman who cares for me, who reminds me the past is not the present. My body, lingering above my precious child, tries desperately to move toward her, to pick up sweet Pamela, but I can't. I, too, am in the grasp of Fear and Sadness. The clutch on my soul, on my very psyche, is so powerful, I can't go to her. I can't rescue her!

My therapist brings me back, having me focus on my breath, look around at and name objects in the room. She speaks to me softly, holding my hands, and assures me I'm safe and this room, where we sit, is reality. It is present.

The rest of the session is a blur. I can't recall much. I'm fixated on the fact that I left my little girl in that vulnerable place of fear, pain, and sadness. I let her down. I abandoned her. In my mind, I committed the cardinal sin. I didn't pick up my child.

34

The Aftermath

I felt that I let my therapist down. I let myself down. I've tried so hard to heal, look at my past, do what I need to do to move on...and I failed. I left her at the farm. I didn't rescue her from the throes of evil and harm! What have I done?

During the twenty-four hours after my session, I obsessed on my failures. I silently crucified myself for being what I thought was a coward. I dared not tell my partner for she too would be disappointed and see what I had done. All this therapy and for what? To walk away.

My mistake, my choice, led me down the dark path of self-punishment. I took my knife and I cut and this one was deep and long. It stung as the blood dripped from the wound. I kept trying to take the guilt and faults out of me. Perhaps, for a moment as I felt the physical presence of pain, I didn't experience the emotions of self-loathing and failure. Then, in a flash, it came back! Even this strategy of self-harm couldn't take away what I did to Little Pamela. Now, I disappointed my therapist, my partner, my friend Barbra, and myself. Again.

I began to think about Dr. Mitchell and the possibility of her ending our sessions together. I figured she'd probably be right to want to do that. How can we continue to work if I can't rescue my little girl?

I imagined my partner walking out on me. Fifty years old and cutting?! Who wants or needs someone around who does that? I imagined my supports slipping away, stopping contact, and giving up on me. I then imagined myself giving up on this healing process and moving on once and forever. Then, I remembered something that happened near the end of my session...

35

The Screen Door

Dr. Mitchell told me from the beginning of our therapy session that I could rest assured that I never had to recall memories to heal from the abuse. She told me that if I want or need to share memories that come, she will listen and help me through them.

In theory, memories don't need to be remembered to heal. That always feels safe to me. It makes me feel believed but without the pressure of recalling memories that might just be more harmful than helpful to talk about. My body knows. My psyche knows. The depth of my very soul knows. It's not having to go to the memory that promotes my healing but rather using strategies, gentleness, and the help of others' love, care, and acceptance that matters. With those things, I can move along my healing path, putting the shame and blame onto my relatives who abused me. They are the rightful owners for this shame.

This is what I remembered in the last part of my session when a terrifying and painful memory bubbled up. At the end of the session, Dr. Mitchell talked to me about developing a strategy that will, perhaps, protect me from the intense emotions of fear, pain, and sadness I experience when in the midst of a memory. She encouraged me to put up a screen between me and the abuse, to protect myself from something

I've already survived and don't need to go through again. She then reminded me that Little Pamela and I are one. She's not abandoned by me but always with me. Too bad I didn't remember that earlier.

I started really thinking about this screen idea. She said maybe a TV screen where you can see it but you don't walk into it. Although I understood what she meant, I didn't like the idea of a TV. For me, I immediately thought of TV as a source of entertainment. I didn't want to watch a "show" of my abuse nor did I want to be in the cast of that "show" of abuse. Instantly, I could imagine it: a Netflix series of *Abuse in the Mennonite Community*, featuring real-life memories and feelings. Yuck.

Yet, I really liked the idea of a screen. I then thought about the idea of adding a screen door to my Bridge at the entrance of the platform to the rest of my life. The screen door would be a barrier between me and the memory and feelings of my abuse. The screen would be thicker wire that has tiny squares between each vertical and horizontal line, so when I look through it, my view is fuzzy. I can see my little girl, I know she's there, but it's not clear what's actually happening. I can barely make out the fine features of her face, let alone the depth of emotion in her eyes. Because of this screen door, I'm unable to connect with the intensity of my little girl.

If I need to, I can open the screen door and see clearly, letting the fear swallow me, and the pain and sadness devour me. But why would I need to do that? By standing at the door, I can still see Little Pamela. I still acknowledge what happened to her, but the screen blocks me enough that I don't embrace feelings and events I've already been through. Perhaps, for now, knowing and using the screen door in my mind and adding one to my Bridge will encourage me to not "go to that place" and experience the pain, fear, and sadness. Rather, if need be, I can look through the screen knowing I don't need to experience that again. Ever.

I like to imagine that, along with the screen door, a solid oak door is hinged there too. Maybe someday, I will close that oak door, knowing that the Bridge I walked over is there but no longer needs to be looked at—with or without the screen door. Right now, however, the screen door is a source of protection I can create in my mind when the demons of my past try to consume me. If I need to, I can paint the screen to make it even harder to see through. The most important thing for me to remember is I'm not abandoning my little girl (she's always a part of me) by doing this. Instead, it's acknowledging we've been through what lies back there, survived it, and no longer need to carry those memories on the front page of our present life story. The memories, fear, pain, and sadness are real, but I don't deserve nor have to go there over and over. I've been there. Done that.

36

When Therapy Changes

Therapy is such an integral part of healing. If I'm certain about anything, I know with my full being I wouldn't be where I am today without having gone through the therapy. My therapist has often said to me that therapy is teamwork; she assists me with the work and healing I do. I can't imagine having to go through this healing without her wisdom, guidance, support, and encouragement.

Therapy is, and certainly should be, a team effort. I don't believe healing can happen alone for me or for anyone. My therapist has countless times said something or suggested something and then I take that idea and make it or transform it into something that further assists me with my healing, thereby adding tools and strategies to my tool box. Honestly, without the strategies she's helped me create or utilize, without these tools that are mine to use when spiraling, I know I wouldn't be living today. That sounds rather radical and extreme but, seriously, think of my past, my patterns, and my depression. It doesn't take a rocket scientist to figure out where my future could have gone.

However, I'm not sure how to *be* now, or what to do when I think of my therapy changing. When I saw the For Sale sign posted on the front lawn of her home where she has her office space, my heart sank. I immediately became afraid of what the sale would mean.

She quickly reassured me when my session started that our appointments would continue and that she would communicate what was happening each step of the way. The uncertainty remained in the back of my mind for the rest of the session.

We continued to meet in her office—a space that had become a safe place for me to cry, breathe, remember, work on healing memories, develop strategies, and find new ways to look at things. I did this with the help of my therapist through the teamwork process.

Her office, her home, our space, was sold within the year of the sign going up. I remember driving up the street and seeing the sign that read SOLD. I felt sick to my stomach and very, very afraid. Questions flooded my mind and I could feel my body regress into a small child, one that feels lost in a great big, lonely world. Again, my therapist addressed the issue, always remaining honest and open with what was going on and about the timelines regarding her plans.

In what seemed like a flash, I was walking into my last session in her office, my safe space. I tried to be brave throughout the entire session and attempted to stay in the moment and not succumb to the temper tantrum that was bubbling immediately beneath the surface of my emotions.

Dr. Mitchell graciously and eloquently led us through our last session in that space, encouraging and reminding me of some of the "great work"—her words, not mine—that I'd done when there. After the session, I remember walking up the stairs to leave for the last time; my legs felt like cement. I didn't look back for fear I would start crying and not stop. I put on a brave face because if I had done what I wanted to, I would have sat on the stairs and—like a small, frightened child—refused to move. I didn't want to leave the safety of that place, the comfort of my therapist, and the change that was coming.

The plan from then on was therapy sessions by phone as she was moving east and will no longer be able to see me in person. I'd experienced a couple of phone sessions with Dr. Mitchell before and, surprisingly, they've gone well. It obviously has a different feel to the in-person sessions, but quickly upon hearing her voice, I find the zone I need to be in when I enter counseling. I don't know when or if I will ever see my therapist in person again. I can't hardly accept that thought. I don't want to either.

When I'm strong and don't feel so vulnerable, I sense the ability to survive our new working relationship. Right now, I'm grieving, knowing she's moved away, and there's a permanent change in my therapy. I'm fortunate in that I can still have phone sessions with her. Many therapists would end their services and refer me to someone else. I will forever be grateful in that I don't need to "start again" with a new therapist after having done such deep and significant work with Dr. Mitchell. I'm lucky she recognizes and appreciates the significance in this change though.

I hear in her words that she's not abandoning me and her move was personal, having nothing to do with me. My little girl wants to scream and say, "Then don't leave!" Grown Pamela wishes her well in this new chapter of her life, wanting nothing but good things and experiences for her. However, right now, in this moment, this therapy change feels very, very overwhelming. Part of me wants to quit, throw in the towel, and surrender to the loss, the change.

It's similar in a way to the darkness, the fear, and the helplessness my small girl child feels. She wants to scream, "ENOUGH!" and just end it all. It feels too hard to face another change—one that's a significant loss.

I'm self-soothed with my adult thoughts reminding me that I can connect by phone and email regularly and team Pam and Terry is not retired, just different. I hear a faint, "It will be alright. We're still a team."

But those dark thoughts beckon me, tantalize me with old coping patterns and ways of dealing with things beyond my control. It feels like this change is one of the hardest things to do. It's hard to even write these thoughts down because they feel so childish and selfish. In saying that, I don't want to use strategies. It's too hard. It's easier to give up, to just end. As each word forms on the paper before me, I'm jolted by an electrifying pain that ripples through my entire body.

I don't know what to do with these therapy changes. I know how I feel. I know the unhealthy things to do. I'm struggling with finding healthy ways to cope. I mean, when I think about it, change has probably always scared me. As a Survivor, I think that makes sense, especially when I haven't had control over the change. I'm healing parts of me over which I had no control or choice when the abuse happened. With that comes fear, uncertainty, for me a fear of being "lost" in the change and the inability to know how to cope.

Those things cause old thinking patterns and behaviors, and those things—although often dangerous—bring comfort and familiarity: a place that has no change. For example, it's way more comforting for me to think dark thoughts or to lash out at my wife when I don't want to talk about my fear or any feeling for that matter, to instead cut and feel temporary relief. Those things are easier for me than to use new or even not so new strategies that may keep my grown-up Pam in control and feeling safe and assured again. I'm at a crossroad and I don't feel safe. Things feel precarious and raw inside of me.

I know what I need to do and what I need to say to myself, but I feel like a big baby who would rather cry, kick, and scream until Dr. Mitchell comes back. But instead of doing any of that, I keep every emotion bottled up inside and I hurt alone. Why? Because for decades I've kept the most profound hurt to myself and I'm quite capable of doing that again.

I wish the end of this chapter brought an epiphany for those of us who experience change in therapy, but I don't have one. I haven't experienced that. In my head, I hear my therapist say, "Yet. You haven't experienced it yet." So, I guess I've some more choices to make and things to think about. I know I'm submerged in my well of sadness right now. Is that okay? I don't even know anymore. What's normal? What's too sad? What's okay to feel? What's unhealthy to feel? Is it normal to not like it when therapy changes, or is that reaction unhealthy? Is it okay to feel like a tantrumming little girl who is afraid, or should I "buck up" and tell myself that life is full of changes?

With therapy changing, I feel like I need to change and I don't know why. I feel like I have to be braver or something, like I can't be vulnerable or honest with how I'm feeling.

Am I the only one who's felt this badly when therapy brings change? I doubt it but I don't know what to do..."Yet."

37

Ups and Downs

Not only has therapy changed, but I've changed a lot since my intense healing journey began in 2016. I feel stronger in some ways and more confident in what I like and don't like—what I'm passionate about even if others around me may feel the same or not. Sometimes, it feels magnificently bold and that I've come to a new level in my development and knowledge as a woman. I feel my Warrior Woman standing tall and strong within my frame and I don't hesitate to speak, feel, or act. It's a feeling that, when I embrace it, can feel as sweet as a kiss or as passionate as two lovers in the night: endless energy and a fire that doesn't extinguish.

That's why it's so hard when those feelings of Warrior strength and passion begin to fade away like the last embers in a fire. I see them flickering and I try to conjure them to reignite but—just like that—they disappear and my feelings of strength, passion, confidence, and power vanish. Just like that, I remember something, I hear something, or something happens, and I'm absorbed back into the body of my little girl. My little girl child, although a Survivor, feels afraid, uncertain, and very anxious that she'll do something wrong.

Lately, I'm also feeling reactive. I'm angry and take everything that

I don't agree with and blow it up, making conversations with me like walking in a minefield. If you're aware, that's not like lighting a match that may burn for a few seconds; it's more like lighting dynamite or stepping on a mine, causing an immediate explosion with shrapnel flying everywhere.

At this moment, I'm tired of trying. I'm tired of feeling like EVERY-THING in my life is affected by my abuse. This spiral of swirling down, sometimes slowly slipping little by little and other times spinning down-ward at a rapid pace, is hard. And exhausting. I've been encouraged to use strategies. I've been told to just embrace the pain: pull it close and hold it tight, imagining it to be a board of nails and, with every sharp point piercing me, stay with the pain and rather than try to "fix" it or make it go away, breathe with it, into it. God damn that to hell! That's why I have a well that symbolizes sadness! I've been holding my pain for decades; with every breath, I feel the intensity of the pain.

Although I've had many Warrior moments, and times of strength and positive thoughts about my healing and future, the clouds aren't parting for me today. The screen door has blown wide open. I've not just met my little girl's eyes with mine; I ran to the Bridge and morphed into her body. Together we sit huddled on a raggedy, narrow, Bridge board, not knowing what to do.

Instead of reaching out, instead of getting help, I resort to cutting. I feel the sting, it keeps me present and, right now, I want to slip into an abyss far, far away. I guess I used a strategy—it's just an old and unhealthy one.

In a healthy child's world, when they fall down and hurt themselves, a little girl runs to a trusted loved one and receives love and comfort. I wish that for me right now. I wish I could curl up on a lap of a loved one and feel comfort. I think my therapist would suggest I can do that for my little girl, and it would be a sign of self-love and care if I did.

I have the power and strength to pick up my little girl, but I have to say, I'm not feeling like it right now. I don't know if it's anger blocking me, or stubbornness, or fatigue, or fear, or what? So, I swirl around in the spiral of healing a little faster at times and, at other times, frozen, hanging on with a white-knuckle grip, unable to move. The question is, do I let go or do I keep trying? History proves that I keep trying but, honestly, I don't remember being this tired, this angry, or this non-compliant.

The ups and downs of healing is like living in a place where one feels as though the ground beneath is one huge trampoline. Sometimes I am up; at other times, I fall down. I suppose as long as my trampoline has springs, I must believe there will always be a "bounce back" under my feet.

38

Being Stellar at Authentic Fakeness

No matter what's going on, no matter how I'm feeling, I've learned to perform—no matter what.

Take today for instance. I feel vulnerable, with tears at the surface. I feel quiet and my head hurts. But my wife and I are having our kids in for our son-in-law's birthday. I can't put myself before my kids. I've been programmed to be fake at the cost of my feelings. Most women have. That's what I did during, after, and in-between the times of my abuse. No one was there to help me, save me, or comfort me. So, I quickly learned to become stellar at faking it. I think girls—most girls—learn this.

When I look at times throughout my life, I think I could've given Meryl Streep a run for one of her Oscars! Add to that my religious background and a society that teaches women to put themselves last, take care of everyone else first, and presto! I'm truly phenomenal at being authentically fake.

Honestly, I think I'm afraid to be real sometimes. Every once in a while, I feel like there's a crack in my foundation and, with enough authenticity, I'd explode with emotion. I'm not talking about a small dam breaking—more like the size of the Hoover Dam in Nevada, United

States!

So, yeah, I write, I express, I feel at least a little, but what is fake and what is real? I suppose the stuff that really hurts is real. The trick for me is to stick with the pain, the feeling, for however long I need, for however long it takes. That's hard because between the fear of never being able to "come back," mixed with the guilt of taking care of me first, stands the powerful feelings of all those memories, all the shame, and all the horror.

The doorbell will ring in precisely ten minutes. The kids are always on time. I'll put down my pen and my sword. I'll shelve how I'm feeling and greet them with open arms; I'll spend the entire visit hearing my daughter talk about her life, struggles, and joys, and I'll be fake about me and how I am. I'll smile, laugh, heap love on my grand-dogs, and look like I'm enthralled with every conversation.

Inside, I'll be crying and screaming. I'll be wishing I was somewhere else—anywhere else. Inside, I will be curled up in a ball making sure that I'm holding onto my feelings tightly enough to not break the dam.

Here it goes. Class 101 for authentically being fake and performing flawlessly. Sit back and enjoy the show...

39

The Switch

I always wondered how trains switch tracks when they go rattling down the railway tracks. I assume that all tracks are now switched with computers connected to the train from the tracks and operate that way. But before computers, how did it work?

When I looked into the operation of how tracks switch the direction in which trains are traveling, it wasn't by chance. My therapist and I were talking about strategies; she suggested that making a different choice is like being on a railway track. When I get to that crucial point of decision making—a healthy decision—which way will I choose to go? Will I pull the switch to go down the healthier track or keep going, following my old thought patterns that may soothe or help temporarily but certainly not over the long term.

This conversation with Dr. Mitchell led me to find two train tracks and put them together but with the option of using the switch. Let me explain.

A railway switch or, *put blade*, allows the train to safely execute a facing-point movement to a diverging path without derailing and crashing. The part of the track that causes the path to diverge is called the *frog*. It's found where the two tracks are set to diverge at the crossing.

The frog ensures the wheels cross to the correct track and keeps them from falling into the gap.

Then there's the guard rail. Two pieces of double track on the railway help the train follow the appropriate track so the train doesn't derail. If the switch or put blades don't work, a signal is sent to oncoming trains. When that happens, it's called *fouling.* The signal notifies all trains on that track to STOP.

After reading about railway switches and hearing Dr. Mitchell refer to the switch, I thought about my journey down the tracks of life as it were. Some days I'm just chugging along, doing life with ordinary and often humdrum activities going on. At other times, it feels like my mind is racing like a speeding train down the track and if I don't take some action to do something, I will derail.

Recently, one of my dear friends died at the young age of fifty-two. Her name was Diane. I experienced a huge loss with her passing. I also thought I was going back to work, but Human Resources had other plans. While these things were happening, I was also dealing with a concussion and with what I think was a broken metatarsal bone in my foot. Life kept happening and picking up speed and I felt little control as I went down this track in my not-so-ordinary, humdrum life.

Black thoughts started consuming my mind: cynical thoughts flooded my head about how cruel life is; I could tell I was heading right for a dark and foreboding tunnel. My thoughts were so fast, irrational, sad, and black as pitch. But just before I derailed, I discovered the railway track analogy and the switch.

I started to think about the direction the track was heading. I had to ask myself whether I was going to slow down and flip the switch—so that when I got to that crucial frog point in my mind, I would be sure to go the right way—or would I ignore the switch and upon arrival at the frog, miss the connection to the diverging path, and fall into the gap?

I needed to ask myself, "What is the frog in my life?" Unfortunately,

I had so many events on my mind—my friend's death, not returning to work, and a concussion, to name a few current issues. These thoughts and events could lead me into a dark gap or hole with no support, no hope, and no divergence.

I think we all have those frogs in our lives. For me, right now, the frog is a crucial place for me to build strength, use strategies, and flip the switch to stay on the right track. The right railway track also has guard rails, which led me to think about this analogy too.

Guard rails keep trains from derailing, ensuring continuous movement down the track. I have guard rails too, if I use them: my safety plan and the people in it are my guard rails. If I access those guard rails, I'm safe from a total and complete life derailment. These two strategies, my safety plan and support people, are the guard rails and main protection that help me from fouling and derailing.

I need to have symbols to remind me and represent analogies or strategies. I like to create things that will help me to pull the switch, so that when I get to that common crossing where I need to decide whether to pull the switch to diverge to the right path or not, I have a visual, right there in my sight.

Railway switches, frogs, guard rails, main protection line, fouling, and derailing or staying on the right track—some of these choices feel like they need to be made minute-by-minute. At other times, I'm chugging along looking at the beautiful landscape around me, not worrying about when the next frog may jump onto my track.

I've executed all parts of railway switching with exceptionality at all stages during my healing. Right now, I'm trying to avoid falling into gaps and becoming derailed if I don't pull the switch. I also need to take advantage of my guard rails.

I imagine myself—today anyway—less and less often derailing and falling into old patterns because of what happened to me as a little girl. Those patterns helped me to survive at different times along the track, but now they don't serve a purpose for survival. They're just habit and have a familiarity that may feel comfortable but keeps me in old thought patterns and behaviors.

It's step-by-step, moment-by-moment, and chug-by-chug, but I need to remember the switch along this track in my life's journey.

40

I'm Not ALWAYS Wrong!

When I look at some of my patterns and the things I want to change, one of them is this almost innate feeling and thinking that when something goes wrong, it's my fault. For me, and perhaps other Survivors, a question I constantly asked myself regarding my abuse was that of "What did I do wrong?" and "Why me?"

Through many intense therapy sessions, I began to actually *hear* my therapist when she'd say, "It was not my fault and I did nothing wrong." By starting to truly hear that, I very slowly began to learn to place the shame I felt back in its rightful place: onto my abusers, which is where it should have been in the first place. I began, ever so slowly, to realize those words coming from my therapist were, in fact, not just words, but truth. That, too, seems to have been an ongoing thinking pattern that needed to be changed. Not just with my abuse, but with, seemingly, so many things. I still find myself going to that old, familiar place with my little girl and asking that question: "What did I do wrong?" I'm starting to hear: "Nothing. I did nothing wrong."

Some days, I say it with such passion and vigor; other days, it comes out like a tiny Mickey Mouse squeak, barely audible even inside my head. I'm hanging onto what my therapist said: even saying it will help me change thinking patterns and, eventually, through my journey, I *will* believe wholly, 100 percent of the time. I wait for that day with anticipation but, for now, I continue to say to myself, "I did nothing wrong."

This thought pattern and the belief that I did, in fact, do something wrong, is in my day-to-day life. When something happens that upsets those around me, I blame myself for their misery and think I did something wrong to make them feel that way. I beat myself up for something that, more times than not, had nothing to do with me but rather occurred because of circumstances, situations, and other people's choices of response.

Some things I blame myself for and believe happened because I did something wrong, are truly ridiculous when I think about them; however, in that moment, they are powerful and real thoughts and beliefs.

I recall a time when my mother was ill so I got groceries for her. She had homemade cookies on the list. I did my best to find homemade cookies in the store, comparing prices, ensuring she would get the "best brand for her buck" (in this case, best cookie). I ended up choosing oatmeal raisin cookies.

When I took the groceries to her place and was unpacking, I showed her the cookies and immediately knew I had done something wrong by the look on her face. She went on to tell me that the kind I got were "Okay, but there are much better kinds at a different store." I went to that place of thinking I did something wrong. Instead of saying something like, "Well, maybe when you host gatherings, your company will enjoy them" or "That's what they had, I did my best," I blamed myself for doing something wrong. Mom even said she was sorry and assured me they would be fine. A few other things were not "correct" with the groceries and even though I did my best and she once again told me that "It will be fine," I could hear none of that. All I heard were the voices in my head saying I'd messed up and did things incorrectly.

By the time I left Mom's place, I was in tears. When I got home, I told my partner what had happened through the sobs and sniffles, and then—with much passion—I said, "It's when things like this happen that I want to cut!" I'd never said that out loud to her before. It shocked me. It shocked me to hear it come out of my mouth, but it was the truth. Inside my head, I was battling the command to go and cut, to punish myself for messing up my mother's groceries.

It was a moment of truth for me. My therapist often suggested that I seem to self-harm when I do something "wrong" or when I think I've done something wrong. I stopped in my tracks. I stopped crying. I stopped everything and I thought, I truly thought, about my therapist's observation. In my head, I responded with something like, "Oh my God. I do take on things, think I did something wrong and then punish myself for the mistakes I make!"

I was proud of myself that day. Something my therapist suggested became a reality in my world—and I did not cut! Let me repeat that: I. DID. NOT. CUT. Rather, I flipped the switch and used my guard rail by telling my partner instead of internalizing all the shame and guilt and have them fester in my mind until I got to the point of cutting.

Here are other examples of this kind of thinking:

- My therapist was selling her home; we'd met in her office for weekly sessions for more than two years. She wasn't just moving but leaving the province and relocating out East. What did I do wrong to make her want to sell and move?
- My friend canceled getting together and I immediately thought, "I did something wrong, so she's avoiding me."

Writing these things down makes it more obvious that this kind of thinking is absurd and exaggerated. Things happen in life that are purely situational and have absolutely nothing to do with what I did or didn't do.

I want to learn to balance my thoughts of feeling good and being happy with realizing that when situations or circumstances happen in life that I may not choose or like, they have nothing to do with me or my actions. I want to learn to not waste my moments of happiness and feeling good with forebodings of what I might do wrong or that something bad might happen that I will blame myself for.

Just like my abuse, I did nothing wrong. The abuse was horrible and life-changing, but I didn't do anything wrong to deserve the assaults against me. I'm not responsible for someone or anyone who sells their home and moves away. I did nothing wrong when a friend canceled our plans because of circumstances perhaps even beyond *their* control. And I sure as heck did nothing wrong trying my best in a grocery store and coming home with oatmeal raisin cookies!

41

What Does It Feel Like?

I've been in conversations with different women who've said things like, "I can't imagine going through childhood sexual abuse!" or "It must be terrible to try and deal with what you went through!" along with other comments.

The one that stuck with me the most was the question, "What does it feel like to try and heal your childhood sexual abuse? Is it even possible?" The answer to those questions would be different each day. The epiphanies bring hope—but the memories and feelings bring a blackness that is indescribable.

A question that has the word *feel* in it has no wrong answer. Feelings are personal and don't make any situation we are in right or wrong. Feelings aren't good or bad or right or wrong. Feelings are based on individual perceptions, experiences, and expressions associated with an event or situation. Therefore, describing what healing childhood sexual abuse feels like to me may be infinitely different from the account of another person who has come through and endured similar assaults, torture, and abuse.

Healing has brought me to the lowest of lows and the highest of highs. Sometimes I'm trudging along in the agony of memories and aftermath of pain—both physical and psychological—for days or weeks. Healing at these times feels like hellfire: a constant burning pain. Most of us have burned at least a finger or other area of flesh in our lifetime. A burn that is second or third degree goes deep enough that it affects our nerves more acutely than a surface burn, which also affects our nerves but not to the severity of a second or third degree. It's difficult to focus on anything else other than the excruciating pain our body is experiencing when our flesh has been burned. When burns are determined to be severe enough, a patient could be put into a medically-induced coma while their burns heal due to the severity of pain and damage their injury causes.

Obviously, I didn't go into a coma with the burning pain I felt deep into my nerves when I began healing my past. When the flames of my past seared my skin, blazed fire into my brain with multitudes of devastating memories, I most certainly felt burning, hellish pain.

I assume that a burn victim must beg for the pain to stop, or at the very least for a reprieve from the deep nerve and tissue damage. I believe people dealing with childhood sexual abuse often get our reprieves from different vices that can be or become unhealthy. Some of these may be smoking, drinking in excess, drug addictions, self-harm, eating disorders, promiscuity, or gambling to think of a few. I'm one of those women who turned to some of those things for reprieve. When the flames were licking at my soul, singeing my psyche, and engulfing my mind, I chose reprieve but not always healthy choices.

When I first experienced the blazing back-draft of memories, I thought I would experience that heat forever. Eventually, the fire became less powerful; the wind that forced its flames onto my body so unforgivingly became less severe and the fire-hot embers of light started to bring some reprieve. How? Some of my beliefs were that if I opened that matchbox and stuck light onto my past, igniting memories,

I would absolutely 100 percent never survive the blaze. But the flames did die down and, eventually, just became smoldering, red-hot coals. They don't disappear or stop glowing with their heat and power, but the flames no longer spread like wildfire over my entire being. The embers bring reprieve; in their warmth and light, they gently flicker waves of hope to the core of my soul.

Surprisingly, as time goes on through my healing journey, the fires are less fierce and the deep nerve and tissue pain is more endurable. I would be lying if I didn't say that sometimes an ember suddenly sparks and the wind picks that spark up fiercely, searing my mind and causing a new memory or old feeling to start flaming all over again. Sometimes I choose old vices to gain reprieve; sometimes I stay with the fire, taking control of the flames and consciously extinguishing them in a healthy and healing way. Each time, the flames lessen, my salty tears eventually stop cascading down my cheeks, and the searing, blazing pain that wreaks havoc in my entire being stops and eventually calms.

Getting to this place, however long, causes me to stand with such Warrior-like fortitude on the highest peak of my life and feel an accomplishment like that of none other! From deep within my belly, I sense a guttural cry, a declaration that in my mind shouts, "I may be burned, scorched, singed, and scarred, but I am victorious! I am on the other side!"

That's how healing childhood sexual abuse feels to me, at least sometimes. The pain is a burning, hellish fire that causes deep nerve, psychological, and physical trauma. But going through those flames has caused me to heal in the reprieve of taking control of the flames; I build strength, gather courage, and feel victories far, far more powerful than the searing memories that engulfed my life for far too long. And I promise, *that* is worth feeling!

42

Moving Forward

Healing has taken me to places deep within myself that have felt so terrifying, dark, and endless. I wasn't sure at the time if I would survive the pain mentally, emotionally, or spiritually. Sometimes it felt like I was in thick mud, unable to lift my foot out from its sucking powers. To take one step and fight against that gravitational force seemed impossible.

I recall asking my therapist things like, "What is the point of this? How is *this* better than before I started therapy?"

She would encourage me by replying, "You will be stronger. You are already stronger" and "You are claiming what is your right to have: freedom from shame and fear." I remember thinking at the time, "Of course she would say that. She is a therapist," then look down at my feet sinking deeper and deeper into the mud and drudgery of healing.

Healing is the hardest work I've ever done. It is the most anguishing, painful, sad—sometimes fearful—act that reaches into the depths of my soul. Healing is NOT quick and easy, but looking down at my feet now, I don't see thick muck engulfing me, trying to swallow me up and devour me. When I look down now, I see solid ground underneath me. I wiggle my toes and feel freedom in my movement. I breathe in fresh air, not the deep murky air that often can be smelled around stagnant, muddy waters.

This healing journey brings me to a different and uncharted territory—and that is *being*. Yep, just being. Pre-healing, I unwittingly lived a very vigilant and fearful life. I was afraid more than I was not. Sometimes, I could name my fear and other times I would get that familiar feeling of impending doom but couldn't put my finger on what that meant specifically.

I've mentioned already how it felt during the deepest, darkest moments of my healing. What I'm experiencing now, WOW! It's completely new. Some days, things are simply ho-hum, almost uneventful except for the usual daily tasks or routines. Those days are new for me in that I'm aware I'm not looking over my shoulder for something bad to happen to me. I'm actually learning to be okay with the ho-hum and simple, uneventful days in my life.

My learning curve now comes with the idea and belief that I deserve good things, exciting things, and wonderful things. I'm working on changing my thinking to "Why not try something new and enjoyable?" instead of living in the fear that paralyzed me many times throughout my life. I'm learning to be content, yet excited, and look toward the future without the "What if something bad happens?" or the "What makes me think I deserve to be happy, financially secure, to do things I like to?" I'm learning which strategies I need to practice and practice and practice.

Thinking differently is also a goal of mine: to stand confidently and do that, even in the hard times when things, people, and events throw me a curve ball and life "happens." I look at my railway tracks and ask myself, "Which way am I going to go?" If I don't mentally "pull the switch," then I find myself with familiar old thoughts such as, "Of course that would happen" or "Bad things happen to me all the time; I shouldn't be surprised." I quickly see that I am stuck in the mud and find things overwhelmingly difficult. Pulling that lever and making the switch is what I attempt to do. I ask myself things like, "Is this truly targeted at ruining me or is this just life happening?" "Is this event or person actually attacking me by making me feel afraid, ashamed, and abandoned?" Or, "Does this have anything to do with me however if I embrace the feelings, it becomes mine?"

Asking myself these questions brings me to a place where I stop and can review what's happened, make sense of things, and move forward, hopefully with the knowledge that I'm okay and will continue to be okay. When I see myself executing those changes in my thought patterns and literally switch, I'm learning to see that I do deserve more than living in fear or with a sense of impending doom.

My feet are now on solid ground. I'm no longer sinking in the mud that tried to devour me with fear, shame, and undeservedness. This ground, the new place in which I am standing, takes getting used to, but it is far better and much more hopeful than where I've been.

43

I'm Different

I'm different, and in so many ways, I feel different too.

It's hard to pinpoint areas in my life where I feel different, but I know I am. I feel more certain about what I like or do not like. I'm okay to let people know those things too and don't feel apologetic or embarrassed by it. I remember not wanting reactions or judgments for things I like or didn't, so I'd just like whatever the people around me liked. Not anymore. Now I'm much better at stating what my likes are and being okay with what I don't like and whether or not those around me are in agreement with me.

With that, I'm working on not feeling guilty with my answers too. I used to feel badly if I liked something that others didn't or if I didn't like something that others did. I'd live in this mental turmoil of wanting others to be happy and if I didn't agree with them, then I was "ruining the moment."

What a paralyzing and, really, selfish way to think! Being caught in the crux of having to make the right thumbs up or thumbs down answer every time someone asked my thoughts or opinions, and on top of that, assuming my answer would destroy the moment or make it better! Like, really??? I don't have that kind of power (does anyone?) and I certainly don't feel it's mine to have. Yet, I exhaustingly lived that way for a long, long time.

It's part of the "pleasing syndrome" that many Survivors and a lot of women have, I suppose. The best part of realizing this is learning that, just like others are not responsible for my state of well-being, I'm not responsible for theirs. For example, I don't have a favorite color. I love many colors and some days I'm more in favor of some colors than others, but I certainly can't point to one as my favorite. There are way too many shades and colors to decide from. No longer do I feel pressured to have a favorite color. When asked, I say, "All of them" or "The rainbow." Most importantly, I don't apologize and no longer feel pressure to have one favorite color.

I'm also different from who I was because I now really enjoy spending time alone. I like being with me and, lately, my thoughts are not too bad to be with either. I sometimes struggle with some guilt when I choose to be alone over going to a family event or gathering with friends. I feel like I may lose connections or they will be disappointed in me, yet I still choose to be alone. For example, when my partner and I were away with her family for the weekend, including most of Saturday, I went to the beach by myself. When I returned, people commented on where I was and that I was missed. I didn't care. I didn't allow guilt to punish me. I loved being by myself and being by water is my most favorite and sacred place to be.

I'm spending time assuring people I'm okay when I'm alone, when the reality is that I'm perfectly content and, currently, most happy when alone. Is it because for so long I spent my life running away from my thoughts and hating who I was so I busied myself almost always so that I wouldn't be alone? I'm inclined to think that, but perhaps there are many answers to that question—many layers I may, or may not, discover right now.

I'm stronger too. Some things that would have devastated me no longer do. When I say devastated, I truly mean the "curled up in a fetal position, rocking, and not connecting with the world around me" kind of devastation! Events, etc., had the power to knock me to the ground and render me incapacitated! This way of coping seems to be happening less and less.

Today I found out I'll be at a new school (again) for the next school year. Although I'm sad, I'm not devastated. In some strange, weird way, I know I'll be okay and will survive the change. My therapist pointed out to me that she has never really heard me talk about the future. I found that comment surprising in that I was not cognizant of that but definitely have to agree.

Lately, I find myself thinking about my future and the different possibilities that could happen for me. Perhaps I'll speak to other Survivors and professionals who would like to know more about healing through creative transformation. Perhaps I'll sell enough of my pebble art to have a partial income that will support my partner and me? Perhaps, just perhaps, I'll be happy...

My head says I deserve that. My belief in that is starting to bloom and blossom into something living and real. I know I'm most definitely in a different place in that even thinking of the possibility is a very different way to view my life. What an exciting place to be! Today I use "exciting" to describe my life and the possibilities for me. Tomorrow I may be fearful—BUT, I might not! Whatever the circumstance, whatever the events or things that may happen, I think I'll be okay. And that is something I really, really like.

44

What was I Thinking?

Just when I think I've turned a corner and feel like the "world is my oyster," devastating things seem to happen. It's not difficult to believe that life happens this way, and it's easy to embrace old core beliefs that life is giving me exactly what I deserve.

I was finally allowing myself the pleasure of starting to think of becoming a grandma, for example. My daughter was sixteen weeks pregnant and all seemed to be going well on her third attempt to become pregnant. Then, at nineteen weeks, they received devastating news that something was horribly wrong with the baby. At twenty weeks and four days, I watched with anguish and pain as my daughter delivered her lifeless baby girl.

Everything about that time was devastating. I could hardly cope with seeing my daughter and her partner go through such a loss. The hopes and dreams of being a grandma were gone. As we said our good-byes to little Isabel Lorianne; no words could adequately describe the sadness and despair we felt. I felt myself losing my belief that I deserve goodness and busied myself with taking care of my grieving daughter.

During this time, I took my pebble art to a store to sell it on consignment. All of my work is there. I remember the pride I felt when I saw it hanging on the store walls and displayed in the front windows. Now, with it being there for about three weeks and hardly selling, I'm starting to have doubts. What was I thinking that my work would sell? What makes me so special? What makes me think I could have a different place and life in this universe?

It feels like when I let my guard down, bad things happen. It feels like I wasn't vigilant and, therefore, chaos consumed me and my family and, in these flames, I don't care if I cut; I don't care about more scars. Why does it matter?

My therapist has encouraged me and challenged me to contradict the foreboding and undeserving feelings with thoughts of "I deserve to feel good" and "Is this an attack on me or a sad event in life that is part of my story but not my life?" She reminded me to stay in the moment.

At least with being on guard and waiting for something bad to happen, I feel prepared and not really happy in the first place. If I don't set myself up with false hope, the fall doesn't happen; even though it still hurts, it can't possibly be as painful.

I am in the spiral again. In the last chapter, I described how different I am, how different I think, and how I look forward to things. In this chapter, life is back to sucking and my thoughts are synonymous with all things negative. It isn't pleasant, but it is familiar. I shouldn't blame myself for things, but I do. It doesn't make sense to blame anyone else. So, when bad things happen, it also makes sense to punish myself.

I'm back to feeling kind of numb, unable to process all inside my mind, my heart, so I push it down. I know that by doing this, I also feel anger, so I push that down too. Every little thing feels huge, so I do very little. If I do anything, it involves taking care of others because that's familiar. I can do it with my eyes closed. If I focus on what is going on around me, what is going on inside of me takes a back seat and it's not as bothersome.

Honestly, I have little energy, so the thought of structuring my day doing "therapeutic" and "healthy" things seems far too exhausting. I can't even identify where my little girl is right now or what she's thinking or feeling. Maybe she got swallowed up in all the drama around me? Does it matter? I can't seem to bring or keep goodness around me so, really, what child deserves that? It doesn't feel safe or welcoming. This place does not have pink, healing energy or a confident Warrior Woman strutting around.

It's at a time like this in my healing when I need to make choices. Do I open my tool box and find a strategy that may work to challenge these old core beliefs or do I allow myself to get swallowed up in this cycle again? I don't think there is a right or wrong answer, but I do think that using strategies is much more effective and healthy.

This time, finding myself in the spiral of healing, I grabbed onto the strategy of writing and I wrote. I wrote and I wrote and I wrote. I was Forrest Gum—but on paper! A lot of what I wrote is in this book. Some things aren't, but the point is *I did not cut*; I did not get to the depths of despair. I listened to my therapist and even though I felt angry at her for not joining my pity party, I thought about the things she said. For example, Isabel is not solely my story: she is Danikka's story. I am affected by her death, but the tragedy is not mine to carry. I can believe old thoughts that life just sucks or I can choose to believe that although something devastating happened, life's not out to get me or my family. It's just life: happy, sad, tragic, joyous, and a myriad of other emotions too.

I can hold on to old core beliefs that want me to think life is not about goodness but rather glitches of goodness and that life mostly is negative and bad things happen to me all the time. Or I can challenge myself to ask things like, "What do I need to take care of myself?" "What do I deserve that feels good?" "Do I want to repair my life, myself, or re-harm?" When I focus on the answers to those questions, then the meaning of "What was I thinking?" changes too.

147

45

High School

I think of my high-school years and feel repulsed. I mostly hated high school. I hated how I looked, how I acted (most of the time), and my home life. High school was, for me, long and arduous. When I think of high school, I think of death and grief.

My mind sees pictures of the boys' faces who were either killed in tragic car accidents or died by suicide. I think of Chuck, Ken, Phil, T. Scott, Michael, Bryan, and Barry. Then, I think of self-harm because I was a teen when I started cutting. I know every secret place to go at my high school to cut or harm.

I think of how much bigger I was than kids my age: bigger by size, height, and weight. I couldn't wear clothes from the stores my girlfriends went to. In fact, I hated shopping. My feet were size twelve women's, so I could rarely buy cool shoes. I felt like an outsider from inside to out.

I never felt pretty. I thought I was ugly, awkward, and desperate. Ugly in appearance, awkward in not knowing where I fit in, and, yet, desperate to fit in and look like I belonged! I mean, think of the terrible things that They did to me. Of course I didn't fit in and if people had found out about those things—OMG!

I had no problem fitting in outside of high school, like at my youth group and the executive, of which I was president, that represented Ontario and Quebec. But high school was painful. I didn't have partners in science. In driver's education, I had a partner who was more of an outsider than me.

I tried hard with drama but could never land a major role because I was too tall, too big, or too whatever. So, I tried being backstage help. It was okay, but I never truly belonged. My favorite thing to do each day was hang out with my English teacher. I enjoyed that more than anything. Every morning I would go up to room 319 and chat with her. That was far better than hanging out in the cafeteria. I hated the cafeteria. I felt like EVERYONE was staring at me.

My parents discouraged my siblings and me from attending school dances. We weren't told we couldn't go but the guilt and message relayed made it clear that it would not be something our parents would support or approve of.

We couldn't afford to buy school spirit wear and I don't think it would've fit anyway. When it was time to graduate, I didn't get photos done. I didn't buy a yearbook. I didn't want to remember, to look back. Ironically, I do remember. I remember more than I wish I did.

Fast forward thirty-plus years...

When I was told I would be transferred the following September to Elmira District Secondary School (EDSS)—my alma mater—at first, I was okay. When I really started thinking about it, I momentarily stopped breathing. I had no idea how I was going to work there without the memories flooding back day after day after day.

I could tell myself that I wasn't that teenager anymore, but I also knew that teenager was in me somewhere. I was aware I was a staff member, not a part of the student body, but I sure wasn't lining up my feelings with that knowledge.

I felt physically ill thinking about how every hallway was a memory—the math wing, for example. A math teacher promised to pass me if I promised him to never take math again. He adored my brother but did not give any thought to casting me away. The English wing reminded me of my friend who had an affair with our grade 11 English teacher as well as one of my best friends; and I remember her boyfriend hanging out at the lockers, me feeling awkward and alone.

I remember my drama class. When the time came for me to share about my summer, I desperately wanted to tell them about my boyfriend and the fun I had with him. I chose not to because I thought they would laugh at me and not believe that someone would have wanted to date me. Other memories came flooding in as well. I remembered the geography wing and our male teacher flirting with all the girls, me being repulsed by it.

I joked around obsessively with my business teacher and must admit that I have some good memories of that class.

Every floor, every hallway, brings back feelings of worthlessness and self- loathing. How am I going to do this? The lump in my throat becomes harder and harder to swallow. The tears in my eyes are harder to blink away. And this is me out of the building, the town, the community! I can't do this! How can I do this???

46

Lavender Land

The day arrived. There I was, sitting in my car, white-knuckling the steering wheel in the staff parking lot at the high school that I left thirty-two years ago for what I thought would be the last time. That morning, the sun shone and the morning dew still glistened on hoods of cars around me. I could hear birds chirping as I opened the window of my car to inhale fresh air. I smelt the familiarity of farm air, the fresh manure that whisks its way into town from neighboring farmland, remembering that it's "fresh" in a different way. I entered the eighty-year old structure as staff, not as a student, but nothing about the moment felt present-day. I was in a time warp with a multitude of memories. Feelings flooded my entire being.

I took a deep breath, grabbed my things, and headed toward the doors that, years ago, I entered and exited hundreds of times. When I walked up the stairs, down the main hallway, and to my office, I tried to steady my heart beat, control my breathing, and regulate my steps. I dropped my things off, saying hi and smiling to those who crossed my path. I wanted my physical demeanor to exude confidence and purpose; on the inside, I felt more like a grade-nine student walking into high school for the first time—a bundle of nerves and high anxiety!

I checked my pockets, pushing my hand deep inside one to feel the smooth pendant that read Warrior. In my other pocket, I had a mound of dried lavender, loaded and ready. I took a deep breath and left my office, prepared for the battle ahead of me.

I turned left outside my door and headed to my old English wing. As I approached the corridor, I noticed it was still the English wing thirty-three years later. I walked up the four stairs to enter the wing; as I passed my old English classrooms and previous lockers, in my mind's eye, I saw the faces of people who'd walked the halls. Walking past each door, I dipped into my stash of lavender, pulled out some, and sprinkled it on the floor; I also sprinkled it by the lockers and at the doorways I used to pass through.

I proceeded down the stairwell to the first floor and basement of the school, and sprinkled lavender onto each step as I remembered being with a friend, laughing and silly, two days before she was killed in a car accident on the way home from Wonderland. I recalled carrying books for another friend who broke her femur because of a hayride accident and used crutches for the next six months of her life.

From the stairwell, I turned right down the tech and math wing. It was still the math and tech wing. I stopped in front of room 31. I closed my eyes and remembered my math teacher almost pleading with me to not take math again and promising me that he would pass me if I promised to never take math again. I remember the incredible relief I felt along with the thoughts of me having to be a REALLY bad math student if a teacher doesn't want to teach me in his class! I poured lavender at the threshold of room 31 and soldiered on.

I walked to the doors I used to enter each morning and dribbled more dried lavender before proceeding to the cafeteria. Going up and down each aisle between the tables, I let lavender flutter from my hand onto the floor. The cafeteria didn't seem as big, and although I could hear the noise from voices in my head, they were beginning to fade. I left the cafeteria with a trail of lavender behind me.

I took a deep breath, pushed the door open, and walked out to the boulevard. The place looked different but felt the same. In the center of the boulevard were new structures and seating areas. And the trees! The trees were beautiful, full-grown maples with branches stretching to the sky, creating a canopy of shade for anyone who walked by.

I went by Phil Luella's, Chuck Rau's, Bryan Martin's, T. Scott Wideman's, and Mike Wilson's memorial trees. At every tree, I dropped lavender on the plaques that proclaimed their names and the dates of their deaths. I wiped away tears when I walked away from those trees that have had longer lives than my friends ever did. I inhaled a deep breath and made my way to the gym.

Fortunately, the gym walls were painted and the portraits of my friends and brother were no longer visible. I dropped lavender on the floor and on the bleachers where I'd sat for countless assemblies and basketball games. The memory of sadness flooded over me when I walked toward the stage. I didn't go into the wings. I didn't stand on the stage. But I threw a handful of lavender under the curtain and walked away. I walked down the "colored corridor"—we called it the colored corridor because it was painted different colors to symbolize different decades—to the small gym, art room, and library. At each place I walked into and through, I left a sprinkle of lavender to reclaim the space that once brought pain, confusion, and sadness.

The library was completely changed: it didn't feel the same, nor did it look like it used to. I dropped some lavender there, just to be safe. I went up the back stairwell and dropped my lavender on each step. I got to the third floor. When I passed rooms where I used to have French, German, Latin, and History, I sprinkled lavender in the doorways.

When I got to my English classroom, I stopped. I smiled and thought of Betty. I thanked God that I had Betty as my high school teacher and dropped an extra portion of lavender at room 314.

On my way back to my office, I stopped at what was once the old guidance department, but was now a conference room, and dispersed some lavender. I scattered some lavender at my science class door, my old vice principal's office, and kept on my way. This exercise, this battle, was a victorious one.

I'd reclaimed, and perhaps claimed for the first time, power in this building. I wasn't the hurting sixteen-year old nor was I the moody seventeen-year old. Rather, I was a strong, wise fifty-one-year-old woman with a lifetime of experience that far outweighed her high school years.

Even writing that and successfully executing *Plan Lavender Land*, EDSS is like a loaded gun to me. I'll continue to need guidance, strength, and Warrior courage to stay in the present and not be saturated with the feelings from my past. The memories run deep, but the lavender has been scattered throughout the building, over the land, and the place has been cleansed.

47

A Letter to My Little Girl

Dear Pamela, Sweet Little Pamela,

I'm sure there were times in your little life when you wondered if you would live through the horror you experienced. Perhaps there were times when you wished you could stop breathing, when you held your breath for *so long* in an attempt to survive the unthinkable acts done to you, when it felt like life was too hard to carry on...and yet, you did! I'm so grateful that, in those horrific times of abuse and torture, you eventually exhaled so you could breathe in once more!

We've been on a journey to get to a place of healing where we can live more days with freedom than with pain. It's been a long and heart-wrenching one, but I have no regrets—and I'm so glad I did it with you.

I must admit, it felt impossible at times, this quest to heal the abuse that is tied to my physical, emotional, and spiritual being. Even with the brilliant guidance and counsel from Dr. Mitchell, at times I didn't think we would make it out alive. And then, sometimes, the memories, the fear, and the physical pain seemed impossible to get through again and I almost found death more peaceful than life. I was close to ending our journey on more than one occasion.

It was a wintry, blowy, and snowy day when I truly saw you for the first time. I was having a therapy session, recalling one of my memories, when I looked down into a dark pit and saw your tiny, vulnerable frame: alone, afraid, and needing to be rescued.

I recall being larger than life and gaining strength I didn't know I had so I could save you from that desolate, dark, and lonely pit. When I picked you up and held you tightly in my arms—your head on my shoulders, your tiny arms clasped around my neck, and your little legs wrapped tightly around me—I felt for the first time ever like I was a whole person, still broken and in pain, yet complete in a way I never had been in my entire life.

I could feel your sweet breath on my neck and your salty tears on my cheek as you moved closer to my face. Your heart beat rapidly from your little chest but slowly began to mimic my heart's rhythm. The longer I held onto you, the more in sync we became. I knew from that day forward I would never, ever let anyone hurt you again. I knew that the significance of the work I did that day with Dr. Mitchell was pivotal in healing some of my past in a way that it could no longer wreak havoc and plant terror in my mind. I knew because I picked up my child.

Thank you, Little Pamela, for not giving up on me, for somehow believing somewhere within your soul there was hope to find freedom. Thank you for surviving. At times, we both chose unhealthy ways to cope with our pain, but the point is, we lived through it. We survived. Together, we survived. Only you can truly grasp what that means when I write, *"We survived."* With each visit from our predator, the acts of violence, torture, beastiality, and sexual abuse were endured over and over and over again.

Despite the pain, suffering, fear, and terror of their acts, we survived.

***

I sat quietly after I wrote that. Little Pamela was in my lap, her white-blonde hair pulled back from her face, her deep blue eyes penetrating mine. We let the phrase *we survived* sink into the depths of who we are. No words were spoken as the tears streamed down our mirrored faces, touching us both to the core.

***

Thank you, Pamela, for believing in me, believing that I could get through this with the assistance and navigation of my therapist and you. Thank you for trusting the process despite the agony, fear, and pain. Thank you for your gut-wrenching honesty and Warrior-like courage to look into our past so we could find freedom today. Thank you, Pamela, for never, ever giving up.

Life continues to have its ups and downs, with gloomy days and days where hope is hard to see or feel. I'm learning that this is normal and, as I learn, I'll teach you, Pamela. Now that we are truly joined together, having come through a grueling hell to cross the Bridge to get to our platform for life, I believe, to the depths of my being, we will never be separated again. I've got you.

Some moments in our healing were monumental in helping us get to where we are today. I believe one the most poignant of those occurred when we heard Dr. Mitchell say, "Of course you were afraid. You had every reason to be." Yes, Pamela, you did. Every reason. And yet, look at us now. We are walking in freedom, dancing on our platform for life to music we create to a rhythm that is unique to us!

Happy, joyful, hope-filled days are bliss! Humdrum days are hard. Either of those days are do-able now with the tools we've found and molded into strategic forces to battle the events that trigger or drag us into the past.

We have these tools, Pamela, because we chose to fight and not let Uncle and Grandfather rob us of our entire life. It's no lie that what they did and took from you cannot be given back. But what we've gained—knowledge, insight, sensitivity, courage, bravery, wisdom, and strength—can never, ever be taken by them or anyone. Ever.

I remember a warm, fall day when I said to Dr. Mitchell, "I want to get to the place when I can say, 'I won, Wilmer and Nelson. I won.'" Pamela, we did it! We have victory and a Warrior's victory to boot!

Sweet Little Pamela. I wish I could promise you the memories are gone, the triggers are defeated, and the healing is complete. But, sadly, I cannot. There will most likely be triggers, possibly more memories, and most certainly, more healing. I do know what I can promise you though. I can promise that, as the woman who picked up her child, I will never, ever put her down.

The future is ours. Together, let's dance, play, create, and move forward, knowing our strength from having survived our past.

I love you, Little Pamela.

With gratitude, Pamela

Postscript

It's important for me to mention that I'm definitely a believer of something far more powerful than me. Whether I choose to call that power Goddess, God, Jesus, Christ, Higher Power, Healing Light, Universe, Willendorf, He, or She doesn't matter to me. In fact, I don't believe it matters at all. God, or the Universe—or whomever—is omnipotent and omniscient enough to handle being called whatever a person can or is willing to identify with. A specific name can often ostracize a person due to their experiences, culture, or past; for example, I believe this power is bigger than ourselves and can deal with whatever name we call that source because, indeed, we are calling on something greater than ourselves.

What does or did God do with the abused? Huge question.

I believe that the Goddess heals if we are open to it. Healing is a continuum, however, and involves a lifetime of work at varying degrees with varying paces. A power beyond me, greater than me, helps me find healing, peace, and freedom when I do the work throughout the journey.

For those who are concerned about my spirituality, you need not be. I am a Believer of something far greater than me and that has remained and will remain a part of me forever. I believe my healing would not have been complete without divine intervention from the Divine.

I hope readers will not judge the words I choose to describe the Great

One but, rather, will accept the message that healing took place in my life and would not have happened—I believe—had I not included Spirit along with the mental, physical, and emotional parts of my journey.

~ Pamela Frey

Contact Me

I would love to hear from you!

You can contact me at this email address
pfrey68@gmail.com

Notes

THE TIME HAS COME

1   Shea, portrayed in the photos in this book, was my constant and loving companion throughout my healing.

TOSSED SALAD

2   https://thoughtcatalog.com/shahida-arabi/2016/09/read-this-during-the-worst-moments-of-your-life/

3   https://blaquemetta.wordpress.com/2020/12/15/a-must-read/

RETRIBUTION

4   https://www.meriam-webster.com/dictionary/retributiononline.

REFRAME THAT THOUGHT

5   A behavioral class in Canada offers programs that will help with social and emotional regulation as well as grade-level education with a smaller student-to-teacher ratio and the support of child and youth workers.

HEALING IS NOT A "TO-DO" LIST

6   Bass, Ellen, and Laura Davis. *The Courage to Heal: A Guide for Women Survivors of Child Sexual Abuse*, 4th ed. William Morrow Paperbacks, 2008. [ISBN 978-0061284335].

CPSIA information can be obtained
at www.ICGtesting.com
Printed in the USA
LVHW021946270423
745343LV00002B/2

9 781777 494001